PEACEABLE REVOLUTION
THROUGH EDUCATION

PEACEABLE REVOLUTION THROUGH EDUCATION

Catherine Cadden

BABA TREE

Chapel Hill, NC

Peaceable Revolution Through Education
Copyright © 2009 by Catherine Cadden

Some names have been changed to protect individuals' privacy.

ISBN 978-0-9825578-0-8

Editors: Sylvia Haskvitz and Jesse Wiens
Cover design and photograph: Jesse Wiens
Proofreaders: Pam Cadden and Jiva Manske

Published by Baba Tree
P.O. Box 508
Carrboro, NC 27510
www.babatree.org

For teachers everywhere – may your passion soar.

For each and EVERY child I have known, with your discipline of heart, deep questioning, magic of truth, courage to be who you are, relentless play, and unconditional love, you are the ones we have been waiting for.

And especially to ALL the TEMBA kids – somehow our walk together continues. It is an honor to know you. Thank you for being.

For all parents who formed TEMBA – who opened their hearts, faced their fears, and pioneered community.

For my family, may you know the nurturance, joy, freedom, and creativity that I have known through these experiences.

For Berne, Glen, Jesse, Jiva, Melanie, and Siréna for the profound integration of laughter, learning, and the sacred.

For Michelle, boots and all of the above.

For a wish – that children everywhere have the opportunity to go to bed safe, free from any violence, sleep soundly through the night, wake to smiling faces who love them, and spend their days free from suffering, playing until the heart tires only from experiencing too much joy.

Contents

Acknowledgments

"It is good to have an end to journey towards,
but it is the journey that matters in the end."

Ursula K. Le Guin

The journey of writing this book is intimately tied to the journey of TEMBA. I feel immense gratitude for the time I shared with each being who offered their wisdom in some way for my benefit and the ever-evolving creation of TEMBA. This includes every child and parent who ever attended TEMBA; every teacher, board member, volunteer, donor, and supporter who made the school a possibility; and Marley, our four-legged devoted German Shepherd who lived out her final years attending to the needs of the children.

This book was made possible by thousands of acts of kindness from innumerable individuals. I would like to offer a deep appreciation for Sylvia Haskvitz, Pam Cadden, Jiva Manske, and Danielle Beenders, for reading these words; offering their suggestions and edits; and giving me love and empathy with each change.

A distinct bow of gratitude goes to the original five families that attended those first meetings and helped launch the school, Ember, Valeri, and Bert; Hudson and Cathy; Megan and Maura; Nitsa and Heather; Zach, Maiya, and Tom.

All the families of TEMBA deserve special mention for their dedication to the school, trust in me, and making it possible to forge new ground in education, which is the essence of this book. I want to specifically thank a few for the "extra mile" they walked with me while on the journey: Kodi, René, and David; Hannah, Dru, and Paul; Cassidy, Trini, and Tim; Ellis, Jo-jo, Anna, and Andrew; Christiana and Elvira; Eve and Sue; Dylan, Amaia, Eleanor, and Mark; Trinity and Brenda; Cadaxa, Mark, and Cheri; Avriel and Mike; Shasta, Gra-el, and Tony; Ellen, Emilia, and Lori.

To the numerous teachers and board members who offered their passion and services to TEMBA, truly, you upheld the authenticity and integrity that became uniquely TEMBA. I specifically wish to thank Berne Fitzpatrick, Jim and JoAnne Saltzgaber, Joe Fajen, Jiva Manske, Linton Hale, Lloyd Barde, Marc Berstein, Siréna Andrea, and Tom Finch for astounding dedication to the process, abiding friendship, ceaseless humor, relentless "showing up", sustaining empathy, and necessary creativity.

Thank you, Julie Green, for being my mentor in Nonviolent Communication[SM].

To Sura Hart for inspiration, friendship and the book *The Compassionate Classroom*. That book lived on my desk as a reference text. It greeted me everyday like a friend, "Good Morning, Catherine. Just a reminder – you can do it differently and it can be FUN!" I believe that book not only forged a path of understanding the application of Nonviolent Communication[SM] in schools but also offered the potential for classrooms to be the launching point for compassionate action in our society.

To Mahatma Gandhi, Ram Dass, Jack Kornfield, Dr. Martin Luther King Jr., Stephen Levine, Ondrea Levine, Nelson Mandela, Happy Orten, Maria Montessori, Rudolph Steiner, Sahn Nicole Hill, Mahriah Blackwolf, Jack Von Dornum, Barbara Pennington, and Joseph Chilton Pearce, for blazing a trail that led me to TEMBA, and offering the spiritual stamina I would need to continue throughout the years. It is my sincere hope that this book honors and carries on your work in some humble way.

To Marshall Rosenberg, whose articulation and creation of Nonviolent Communication[SM] gave me inspiration, clarity, and understanding, I thank you for your influence and presence in my life. Your work has given to all a tangible way to communicate the truth that lies in our hearts.

To Gloria Cooper, a very special thank you for being the first person to ask and encourage me to take pen to paper and bring to life the philosophy of education that would be the breath of TEMBA. You, R.D., and the New Age Academy rooted my passion and vision with your trust, appreciation, compassion, and beauty. Gloria and R.D., thank you for your unwavering faith in me.

There is one family, the Roney-Janssens', who has been with me on this journey from before the philosophy was completely written, through the actualization and the lifespan of the school, to the epilogue of manifesting this book. Throughout all these moments, I appreciate that we strived to live the relationship of the sun and the earth that Hafiz describes: *"Even after all this time, the sun has never said to the earth – 'You owe me.' – Look at what can happen with a love like that, it lights the whole sky."* With tears of awe, giggles of "what did we do?", and a heart full of love I offer gratitude to Michelle, Montana, and Glen; you are family. Without you three, I wonder if there ever would have been a TEMBA.

To my partner Jesse, for his ideas and kindness. Beyond the technical aspects of design, formatting, and dealing with my lack of willingness when it comes to computers, Jesse was, at times, my confidence and faith that this was a meaningful project that needed to get out to the world. This book could never have been completed without his love and caring support.

Finally, to Tosh, thank you for being, giving your brand of fuzzy empathy to all, and willingness to dog for your needs.

Foreword from a TEMBA Teacher

Jiva Manske, M.A.

T he first time that I stepped into the TEMBA classroom, I was
struck by a strange sensation that I could not name. It was more
than the joy of seeing happy children playing together or the comfort of
coming out of the snow and into a warm room. It was a sense of ease and
peace that came over me as I looked at the colorful, art-filled walls of the
small schoolhouse, and listened to the quiet music playing in the
background. I walked through the spacious room, past a small round
table, and up the stairs as my eyes swept over the geometric designs that
students had meticulously created and hung on the walls of the stairwell.
To the left of the top of the stairs was a tree made out of paper, with words
that I immediately recognized as universal human needs printed on each
piece of bark, and words that represent feelings on each of the leaves.

Underneath the tree were drums of all shapes and sizes, including a round gathering drum painted with bright figures on its side, delicately crafted *djembe* and *djun-joun* drums, and smaller hand drums, wood blocks, and bells. Past the tree, on the ceiling above a large, thickly woven rainbow of an oval rug was a paper spiral, a timeline that began with a huge explosion and traced millennia of geological, biological, and finally human history as the coil curved around the tops of the room's four walls. The dates were marked by pictures of men and women who had contributed to peace throughout history, indicating birthdays of people like Thich Nhat Hanh and Elizabeth Kubler-Ross, and moments like Rosa Parks' historic refusal to move to the back of the bus, and the Gandhi-led Salt March. The birthdays of each of the children in the school were also bunched together on the timeline, separated by the small expanse of six years that separated the oldest from the youngest.

What I quickly realized, even as I joined Catherine and the children sitting in a circle on top of that rainbow rug, was that each of these objects were all placed with a purpose. Everything had been created with a careful eye toward constantly reminding those in these rooms of their connection to and interdependence with beings present, past, and future. Further, because everybody's work was represented throughout the schoolhouse, all knew that they had contributed to the beauty in their world. Amidst daily activities that included learning to read and write, doing mathematical calculations and scientific experiments, speaking Spanish, singing songs, and playing instruments, those in the classroom also practiced being a part of a truly peaceful and just community. When students created the sacred geometry I saw on the walls, they simultaneously practiced creativity and critical thinking, and also explored the language of the universe, uncovering the truth of unity, the birth of connection, and the building blocks of life. Similarly, the drums were not only used for group connection and self-expression, but also were a constant reminder to respect the link to other students who had passed through the TEMBA community. The timeline above our heads was a testimonial to interdependence and the power to create new directions for the world as it traced a history of the culture these students were striving to embody.

Over the next 15 months I felt myself merge with this culture, at first simply bearing witness to the pitter-patter of feet running through the school house and the laughter and tears that happened every day, and later fully immersing myself into the circle. I had arrived with the intention to stay for a few weeks, having recently completed a master's degree course that focused on peace education, and hoping to understand more directly the concepts that had filled my books, my term papers, and my head for the previous year. Perhaps inevitably, I stayed longer as I found myself initiated into the group one morning when a conflict sprang up to envelope parents, teachers, and students alike. Asked to facilitate a restorative circle between a group of students, I was struck by the ease with which my simple presence was supportive; I said almost nothing as these people, at the ages of 7, 8, and 11 each held the space for each other to go deeply into the pain that had ruptured into disconnection, and quickly came out the other side with tangible agreements and strengthened bonds. After two more circles that day that included more members of the community, I found, quite suddenly, that I had already joined Catherine and her cadre of little colleagues, who were all explicitly focused on becoming peacemakers in their world.

I spent many of the following days and evenings in awe of the space that had been created, which seemed to embody partnership between people whose power I had always experienced to be totally out of balance due to age. 6 year-olds and 12 year-olds worked and played together. Children and teachers facilitated projects and conflicts together. More than that, it seemed that simply walking into the schoolhouse, a different way of relating to each other emerged, supported not only by the arduous task of constant personal responsibility, but also by symbols, rituals, and practices that created a structure and a safety net when someone slipped and fell, physically or emotionally.

And there was a lot of slipping. This was not a tranquil, utopian bubble in which everyone always got along. Yet I found that after the hardest days I felt most alive, as I grew ever more aware that conflict, when fully engaged in the present moment, can lead to profoundly authentic connection. This built trust that I, like the younger members of this learning community, could be who I am, no matter what. I didn't have to always be gentle and kind and loving and perfect to be the person or the peacemaker that I dreamed of being; I found acceptance for both the light and the dark places within myself, and through embracing the uncertainty that came with every day, I grew in my own ability to contribute. The collision between conflict and learning that I both observed and experienced at TEMBA was intense, and I came to more fully understand that learning does not necessarily have to look a certain way, with activities and curricula, and instead can come at any moment in life.

In fact, what I participated in was an environment where life and learning were intimately integrated. In the midst of all of this, the amount of learning that was happening was staggering. As Catherine often jokes when telling stories of students who have gone on to public high schools and are now beginning their lives as college students, an unforeseen side-effect of TEMBA is good grades. Those who come through TEMBA discover not only their love of learning, and their own creative spark, but are nurtured to truly believe that their voices matter in the world, and that they can contribute to themselves and the people in their lives.

Beyond any of the teaching methods, activities, projects, or practical tools that Catherine has developed over the years, what stands out to me is her commitment to co-creating a space where ideals of interdependence, peace, and community are already realities. She carries an awareness of that space with her, without the frills and fuzzy softness that can be nauseating to those less idealistic than myself – connection is here, lurking, even in the darkest, dankest, most remote and scary places in this universe. From a small-town schoolhouse to the war-torn and dusty roads of Kabul, from the flowing movements of a dancing lodge to the strain of carrying a backpack amongst the highest peaks in North America, I've walked with Catherine as she has experimented with truth. What I've come to realize is that what she does is simple: she follows her heart, and expects nothing but the same from those around her. She has certainly supported me to follow my own, and I know that with this book, she hopes to inspire you to follow yours.

— Jiva Manske, M.A.

European University Center for Peace Studies

Teacher at the TEMBA School

Foreword from a TEMBA Student

Hudson Sadlier

TEMBA was my first introduction to such a diverse variety of subjects, compared to the traditional public school I attended for 1st and 2nd grade. From what I can remember back when TEMBA was nestled in an old church/school called St. Vincents, I was learning Karate; dance; art, including geometric art; fiction writing; traditions of Native Americans, as well as all the basics a school should have.

Everything I learned at TEMBA made me crave knowledge. Children grow up now with schools planning for them to be accountants or retail clerks, or business CEOs, when what we really need are more artists and musicians, theoretical physicists and biological researchers, directors and photographers. Even if they choose to become CEOs, it will give a new outlook on the world we live in, which in this time period is much needed. TEMBA gave me, as well as many of the other kids who attended, a thirst of knowledge – beyond just wanting to be the manager of a big corporate company. TEMBA made me want to find exactly what it is that we want to pursue – to always try something new instead of repeating what has already been done.

This thirst for knowledge is also mentioned in Plato's Republic. In the book, Plato attempts to define the perfect city. When the subject of who will want to rule this kingdom comes up, Plato uses the term "Philosopher King." In the traditional sense, a philosopher is considered someone who is obsessed with logic, reason, and theories about different abstract ideas. But the "Philosopher King", as Plato describes, is someone who loves knowledge, not just the abstract. They want to know everything, astrology, math, art, sports, etc. I feel that exposing us to such a variety of subjects to learn, TEMBA created a group of philosopher kings. Because each one of us experienced so many different kinds of knowledge at TEMBA, we are beyond that point where one feels overwhelmed by the difficulty of learning a certain skill or subject. We have gotten to the point where we know the basics, and now we want more.

Personally, TEMBA has made me a musician by exposing me to different instruments at a very early age, some of which some eighteen-year-olds didn't even know existed. TEMBA made me into an artist by showing me how to create art out of geometry. And now, while people around me in my college level art course struggle to grasp the concept of how to draw a cube, I can do it with ease, and while they dismiss the course as just a requirement, I see it as an opportunity to advance my knowledge of drawing beyond just cubes. Because of TEMBA I can program computers, play multiple instruments and compose music, draw and paint, as well as many other skills I have accumulated over my life because TEMBA showed me the power of learning new things.

Ultimately, TEMBA has taught me to love knowledge no matter what form it might come in, even if that form might be something unfamiliar, uninteresting, or even dangerous, because trying new things is the only way to know whether they are worth trying or not.

— Hudson Sadlier, *a.k.a "Big Fuzzy"*

Sophomore, Seattle University

Student at the TEMBA School

1997 – 2001

IMAGINE!
IMAGINE WALKING INTO A CLASSROOM WHERE
EACH STUDENT IS FULLY PRESENT IN THEIR OWN
ESSENCE. THEY ARE AT TASK WITH WHAT THEY
HOLD VALUABLE. THE BUZZ IN THE AIR REFLECTS
A DEEP SATISFACTION WITH AN EXCHANGE OF
OPEN MINDS. THE PHYSICAL ENVIRONMENT IS
CREATIVE, CARING AND LOVING. EMOTIONS ARE
NO LONGER SUPPRESSED BUT INTEGRATED. THE
EDUCATIONAL PROCESS ADDRESSES THE WHOLE
HUMAN BEING, OVERCOMING ANY
FRAGMENTATION. CHILDREN NO LONGER
EXPERIENCE EDUCATION AS SOMETHING THEY
MUST SURVIVE. THEY ENGAGE LIFE.
THEY THRIVE!

INTRODUCTION

❧

A Funny Thing Happened on the Way to the Bathroom

"True compassion is more than flinging a coin to a beggar. It comes to see that an edifice that produces beggars needs restructuring."

Dr. Martin Luther King, Jr.

Autumn air. A sea of asphalt. Over a hundred children crying, bellowing, screeching, laughing. I stood my post on the public school grounds. I was working the quadrant near one of the swing sets. I needed to go to the bathroom.

I dared. I left my post. I walked quickly to find relief. I arrived at the door of the little girl's room and realized I can't go in – I'm a teacher. I must go to the teacher's bathroom, completely on the other side of the schoolyard behind two other buildings near the nurse's station where the children line up to take their Ritalin.

One of the rules at this California public elementary school was that no teacher was allowed in the children's bathroom. It was a rule created because of the fear of sexual abuse. I was irritated with the idea that I could not relieve myself in the closest bathroom to my post, and the implication that somehow I was guilty until proven innocent. I began to wonder, "Does not allowing teachers and children to share bathrooms really stop sexual abuse?" I guessed it offered some sense of protection but, did it really end the possibility of it ever happening again? I have always been most interested in solving problems completely rather than placating people or situations for the short term.

Why do teachers have to stand guard over children during their free play anyway? Oh, yeah, it's because children now bring weapons to school and open fire on one another.

Why am I to assume that children will do things to hurt themselves or each other so I better be there just in case? It's because children imitate the adults in their lives and by age 7, in the U.S., children have witnessed over one million murders on television, film and video.

Why couldn't I be in "ear shot" in my classroom preparing for class and then they could come get me when needed? Oh, yeah, I was trained in the credential program that children are to be "supervised" constantly because they are "too young" to know better.

I did not become a teacher to be a guard for student's behaviors in the yard.

Then I began to think about the 'No Hug' rule in our school district. 'No Hugging' meant that no one at school was allowed to hug. This rule had been created so that there would be no touching of any kind. The thought was that if students aren't allowed any physical contact then this could avoid fighting as well as any confusion about touch between people. I wondered if no signs of affection really were useful in educating our children. Could they really learn with simple nurturance removed?

I began to think about the Junior High down the road that this school feeds into and the students I knew there. The students had to view hugging as a misdemeanor, an activity to covertly sneak in between classes. I also thought about how these students now all had to carry all their belongings with them constantly because lockers had been removed to prevent them from hiding anything illegal. Truly, we were living out the old adage that children can't be trusted and should be seen and not heard.

I looked around at the children on the schoolyard in front of me.

I wondered if more and more rules would really teach these beings how to get along peacefully. I wondered if offering more and more restrictions to their freedom of choice really assisted their learning. I wondered if more regulations really supported teachers to teach.

In that moment, I woke up. I mean I really woke up! This playground is the microcosm of our society. What we witness here are the small doses of what is happening in our world. What we witness here is what will eventually happen in our world. If we truly change how we educate we could actually change how our world functions.

I have heard adults, myself included, discuss their childhood experiences from the playground as battles fought well and survived. I have witnessed child after child come to school with a full plate of turmoil from their home life only to be punished for behaviors that the administration defined as "disruptive", or ridiculed on the playground for befriending someone in the "wrong" crowd (you can substitute what word works here for your district: gang, group, clique, etc.). When these are the experiences afforded our children, we need to ask ourselves, are we supporting violence and war in our world by simply employing our children to practice victimization, hatred, and antagonistic defensive behaviors from day one at school? In that moment, I felt despair because I wanted so much for a different outcome, for the children, for all of us.

Now absorbed in thought I returned to my post. The thing about being a teacher is the urge to go to the bathroom leaves just as soon as you've distracted yourself. This might be why teachers have the highest bladder infection rate in the United States.

"What if…?" I began to wonder. What if we create schools where students had a real opportunity to practice compassion, equanimity, and conciliatory behaviors? What if the focus was not on controlling or managing children but a focus of trust so that learning could happen together as a community? What if we create a microcosm of a society where every day has the potential for people to experience a harmonious, productive, equal and joyful world?

I decided in that moment that it is vitally important that we educate in a way that offers children an opportunity to practice peace. I decided to start a school.

That was 1993.

As each year our children are subjected to more diagnoses with medications; taught more 'standardization', militarism, classification, racism, and materialism; exposed to more and more violence that actually threatens their very lives, I am deeply curious why we are waiting for the system to change when we have all that we need to create the change we wish to see. The hard part is not in convincing people that change is needed; the challenge is in activating people to make the change, and having it happen peaceably.

From my perspective there were and still are many systems and laws worth changing, with how we educate at the top of my list. So when I first read the work of Henry David Thoreau, in particular *Civil Disobedience*, I was delighted with the concept of a "peaceable revolution" to change systems. This idea of bringing peace and revolution together strikes a deep cord in my heart. Thoreau describes it as a revolution taking place through "peaceable" actions by the people who no longer desire to go along with doctrines, systems or laws that do not serve humans.

Mahatma Gandhi's nonviolent movement in India was inspired by Thoreau's idea of a "peaceable revolution". Gandhi shared in his teachings that nonviolence is not the mere abstention from violence; it is about building relationships between human beings. Because I believe education happens as a result of relationships, Gandhi's writings, especially on education, were a great influence in the development of my philosophy of education. I truly believe we can design educational systems that spark a revolution of peace for our entire world, inspiring the creation of ideas, systems and laws that serve human needs.

This book offers my personal odyssey as an educator, and as a human being – what I have learned along the way and what I hold valuable. It is the journey of children I have met that have "shown me the way" on this path of education, peace, and revolution. Within this book are just some of the numerous experiences from TEMBA, the K–8 academic school that I started in 1997, to ignite peaceable change in our world. It is an adventure that includes travel as far as off as Afghanistan and as near as my own heart. These are real-world stories for anyone who longs for peace on our planet, with tangible application to one's classroom, community, family, and life.

However, I want to be entirely honest. This is not a "how to" book in the usual sense or even a writing that will suggest that what I found is the "right way" to work with children. I simply want to offer the stories of the experiments that I have tried and share the results that I have found. I hope for you to decide what you like, what you'd like to learn, and what you will leave behind that does not fit for you. Peace can happen, starting one student at a time. My dream is that if we restructure our schools we can restructure our society. With the heart-full, empowered, compassionate choices of the people who attend these schools, I believe we will know what it is to live in peace in our hearts, in our homes, and on our planet. I want nothing less than a "peaceable revolution" through education.

1

Sink and Swim

"Real education consists in drawing the best out of yourself – what better book can there be than the book of humanity?"

Mahatma Gandhi

Eighteen years old at the University of Kansas my earliest introduction to formal teaching was a system called 'Behavior Modification'. The sole goal was to get students who were labeled autistic or learning delayed to do what was being asked of them, through a punishment and reward system. In one study we were shown how candy was effective as the reward if a student showed the 'appropriate' behavior. A teacher would give candy or praise if the student did a desired behavior. If the student did not perform the behavior, candy was removed or the teacher would stay silent with no interaction with the child. Large graphs of the student's behaviors were created to track and judge the student's performance. Once a student performed a set of behaviors correctly then a new set would be introduced. The behaviors taught were based on what teachers and administrators thought would be possible of that particular student if they could be put to work later as an adult.

I felt such a connection to the children I witnessed. I honestly wondered if being 'well-trained' was going to really satisfy them in their lives. I just couldn't imagine happy children living in confined circumstances where others decided their fate of opportunity. In one of my regular class outbursts, I shared my disbelief that any of this teaching was useful to humanity and then asked the professor about an idea I had been rolling around in my head.

> *"Even a very young child realizes that behavior management systems are not intended to foster curiosity or creativity or compassion: they are primarily designed to elicit mindless obedience..."*
>
> **Alfie Kohn**

"I am not confident that children raised with this program will really be happy. I am curious about the possibility of building an honest loving connection with the student to develop an internal motivation for learning. Wouldn't the child be happier if they were connected to the task they were doing and actually wanted to do it rather than be placed in situations where they have no choice?"

He grimaced, " This IS the most loving way to deal with these types of people." And continued his lecture. In that moment I began to sink in a sea of doubt. I didn't see the benefit in the separation teachers make from their students by seeing the student as a diagnosis to be dealt with or an object to be molded.

I dropped the class.

Committed to changing the world one two-year-old at a time, I took a job as a Pre-K Room Teacher studying to become a Kindergarten Teacher. It was my first actual teaching job. I was so excited to be on the path of teaching and doing it differently. I was working at a Montessori school in Kansas City, while still at the University of Kansas.

What I remember most about that experience is the warm wooden counting blocks, a student who used roaring like a lion as a primary mode of communication, and the discovery that no matter how cozy a room is, the teacher truly is the biggest influence on the students.

In Montessori schools, the general idea is that children can self-motivate learning. In my days as a student teacher, I took in the vulnerability of the students. I observed the wonder of children trying brand new things, exploring possibilities, engaging in learning every moment. I also saw firsthand how teachers offered feedback that there was a 'correct' way or a 'correct' answer.

> *"A teacher affects eternity. No one can tell where the influence stops."*
>
> **Henry Adams**

When students would express emotions, they were "shushed" and then reprimanded for their behavior. Students tried different communication styles and then would get sent to the principal's office. When students found themselves in conflict, they would get sent to "time out", a chair in the corner of the playground or classroom. I witnessed ways a child's willingness to learn could get turned off. I was confused that something may have been lost in translating Maria Montessori's work.

Maria Montessori considered 'attacking the mistake' and 'reprimands' as useless. She wanted to work with supporting the 'natural evolution of voluntary action'. I found I agreed with her. She too, wanted education to inspire peace.

Just a few years later I met Aaron. An electric reactor stuck on pause is the best description I can give for my first impression of this eleven-year-old boy. Aaron was diagnosed a "non-verbal autistic" and had a full behavior modification program with another teacher in the hopes of being "mainstreamed" into the local public school. His parents hired me because someone they knew recommended me as a student teacher from San Francisco State University (SFSU) who taught dance to children. I was to supplement his "program" with movement and music.

With a tinge of youthful arrogance, I stated up front, "I don't believe in behavior modification."

They agreed to have me teach him in my own way, probably out of sheer curiosity to see if I could get Aaron to cooperate. Our sessions would take place in the recreation room of their home.

My first session with Aaron went like this:

"Hi Aaron!"

He looked past me, continuing his rocking back on forth.

"My name is Catherine."

He looked past me, continuing his rocking back and forth.

"I am here to dance with you or drum if you like."

He looked past me, continuing his rocking back and forth.

I have to admit, at that moment, I swelled with doubt and the thought that the professor in Kansas might have been right and I was overly idealistic.

I put on some music.

He brought his hands to his ears and began rocking side to side. He didn't seem to be enjoying it. I turned off the music. I took his hand and invited him to sit down. I sat with my back pressed up against his back. I could feel his rocking motion. It was extremely soothing. I felt lulled into a meditative state. We sat for the remaining 50 minutes of our session.

And that is exactly how the first two months of sessions went. A simple attempt on my part in the beginning ten minutes to invite Aaron to participate in something I brought, then we would sit and share the silence of his world. I learned his rocking patterns. If the rocking slowed with long pauses between the back and forth he was content, calm and connected. When the rocking quickened to the point of making Aaron seem invisible and when his energy radiated out to the walls of the room, he was fully in another world – absolute bliss. If I closed my eyes I could see colors that seemed to be created by the rocking motion. Although I was getting quite an education on the inner dimensions of a being who walks in the world labeled autistic I couldn't help but think that I wasn't doing my job. I mean, after all, I was hired to dance not sit. The doubt swell became a tidal wave.

I decided that I would ride the wave! My conviction was to take charge the next session and really focus on "getting" Aaron to move his body. I walked through the front door of the house with determination dripping from my pores. If I had been a bit more self-aware at the time I am sure I would have felt embarrassed by my parade.

"Hi, Catherine," Aaron screeched, his hands waving and a smile smeared across his face!

Now *I* was "non-verbal".

His mom then shared that he had been using his words and was verbal a lot more since my sessions with him. She thought I knew.

Aaron's parents and previous teachers had considered him nonverbal because at age five he had stopped making sounds that anyone could understand. They were delighted with how much he had been coming to life, using words and hand gestures, since I started working with him.

The tidal wave crashed. I was now being dragged by the undertow along the rugged oceanic floor of doubt. Learning to swim is one thing, but really learning to sink is another. What did I do exactly that contributed to his breakthroughs? I sunk. I sunk into continuing not knowing what to do next.

> *"There is nothing like looking, if you want to find something. You certainly usually find something, if you look, but it is not always quite the something you were after."*
>
> **J.R.R. Tolkien**

From that day on, we spent our sessions with the first half hour completely immersed in the silence Aaron liked to keep and the second half hour singing, dancing, drumming and learning Sign Language.

He continued to choose to be primarily nonverbal. Over our first year together he learned enough sign language to be understood by others and to have conversations. A program was created at his school so his classmates could learn to Sign to communicate with him.

Aaron taught me that being heard and being understood are vital for connection and learning. A student builds trust when the teacher's primary intention is to connect authentically. A student engages a willingness to learn when there is an authentic connection rather than an agenda to comply with.

My journey with Aaron revealed to me an important secret for my life's work. It is the same secret that my friend, Dominic Barter, learned creating restorative justice circles in the favelas of Rio de Janeiro, a place where murder is the number one cause of death for children. Dominic shared it this way with me, "I don't have faith. I have doubt. And that's it really."

That's the secret: to have doubt. Faith is an unquestioning belief that needs no evidence or proof. In my world, in every job I have chosen working with children, including starting my own school, everyone expects evidence or proof that what you do will work. In every step I have taken in life, particularly my work in education, I have done so with a questioning belief – not sure that what I do next will work. I forget who said it first but truly, we may be able to question the power of faith, but it is harder – I think impossible – to question the power with which we doubt our faith. So, when doubt rises, I sink. I let it capsize me completely. Letting go, something much more powerful than my own self-will takes over and doubt becomes the trust that I can actually swim. Being honest enough with myself that I can have doubt in what I am undertaking or what I am trying actually ignites a confidence to attempt swimming – to try new things with my students. Life is a vast ocean of doubt out there, and luckily, I love to swim.

> *"The most beautiful thing we can experience is the mysterious."*
>
> **Albert Einstein**

Near the end of my studies at San Francisco State University (SFSU) I found myself working in California public school kindergarten classrooms. I was assigned as an assistant to watch the "bad" students who had been acting out. The principal wanted me to monitor these kids so the teacher did not have to take time from "teaching" to deal with them. I was about to get more swimming lessons.

The teachers and the principal in this public school so emphatically described Bobby as a hitter that he was referred to as "the hitter" rather than Bobby, even by the students. This label would be written in a file that would follow Bobby throughout his educational career. This label made him a candidate for medications.

When I met Bobby I did not meet a "hitter" or a "bully" – I met a five year old.

During class we had 'reading time' where our choices were to listen to *Little Red Hen* on tape or to look at another book. Bobby was moving from choice to choice unable to decide what he really could focus on when he went for a chair with someone else in it.

Bobby balled up his precious little fist ready to strike a blow. I caught it mid-flight in my hand. Doubt rising in me, I wondered if what I was trying would work or instead get me my own reprimand. I stopped his hand mid-stream to interrupt what he was about to do. I didn't want him to hit again because the punishments he received in this school weren't giving him what I thought he really wanted, which was connection. Can you hear the waves crashing around us?

I uncurled his fingers and began to sing the sound "OOOOOO" into his hands, which were now cupped in mine. During that time of student teaching I had been working on my voice with a teacher, Sahn Ashena from The Sound/Movement Integration Center. She was helping me learn to open and have confidence in my own voice. In sessions with her I moved from a year of silence to making simple vowel sounds, then letting them elongate and blossom into fuller expressions. When I had Bobby's small hand in mine I was touched by the effort it took to hit and imagined how much must have been inside of him, like myself, which desired expression. I simply tried the tool I had handy in the moment, singing a vowel.

He looked shocked and said, "What you doing to me?"

I swallowed, still floating in doubt, "I'm putting magic in your hands – would you like more?"

"Use the light that is in you to recover your natural clearness of sight."

Lao-tzu

He said, "yeah," feebly but with willingness to dive in the water with me. I sounded a little more.

When I sensed both of us above water I said, "O.K., here's the deal Bobby, and I'm guessing you're really frustrated that it is so hard to find the words to tell people how you feel?" His eyes fixed on mine. "I want you to make a pact with me – anytime you feel so frustrated that you think the only thing you can do is hit, you come running, find me and I'll sing magic into your hands. O.K.?"

He agreed. We shook hands. He sat down in an empty seat with a book, sounding out vowels.

Two days later on the playground, Bobby came running up to me yelling, "SING! SING!"

I took his hands in mine and sang into his hands. He started to cry. He started to explain how much he missed his mommy and how he wished she would come home. He had a fear of trusting that things would turn out all right. He felt anger about his parent's separation.

Bobby stopped hitting. He had been using hitting as a strategy to express his pain. He stopped because what he really needed happened – a compassionate understanding – a connection where he could share what was going on for him.

31

Bobby taught me that it is impossible to think a child can place their emotional body to the side so that the educational day can run "as planned". I discovered that to observe a child is not to assess the child, but to bear witness to their unfolding process so I can offer careful attention to what I see or hear them do. I discovered that to be with another human being, especially the beings I would label my students, in a non-judgmental state offered an authentic connection that builds trust. It validates their reality and invites them into the process of learning.

I often hear teachers tell me they don't have time to build connections with students because they have to get through course material. What I saw and continue to see are teachers who burn out and who are undervalued while students struggle to be seen and heard.

Everyday we, teachers, enter the classroom and meet whole human beings. When we ignore what is alive in us while trying only to engage the intellectual processes of the students we automatically invite rebellion.

What is alive in each individual in the classroom is an authentic presence. This authentic presence alive in us, the teachers, wants to connect to the authentic presence inside each student. It has been my experience that with this connection between the teacher's authentic presence and the student's authentic presence, learning happens in an effective, efficient and joyful way. It engages the whole human being and opens that learner and teacher to the limitless, creative, life-long process that is the essence of learning.

If we can be with the child in their reality while simultaneously inviting them into our reality, we have infinite possibilities in learning together. When we only force them into the reality that we have decided "is best for them" then we not only limit their potential but we run the risk of losing the gift that they are wanting to develop and give to us.

Johnny drives this point home.

In his file, Johnny was "learning disabled". I was an aide and my task was to help him focus. I met this six year old. My immediate impression of Johnny was that he had bright eyes, the kind that suggested there were whole new worlds behind them.

Johnny was definitely moving at a quicker pace than others around the classroom. We all were instructed to go to the library for library class. We all marched over in a line. I was holding Johnny's hand to assist him in his position in line. In the library we took our seats on the floor. The librarian began to talk about how a library works. Several butts began to wiggle (remember we are all five and six years old) but Johnny began to stand up, sit down, stand up, sit down, stand up, etc. This was definitely not pleasing to the librarian, nor supporting anyone's ease in paying attention.

Diving into deep water, I whispered to Johnny, "Would you like to take a walk outside?"

He yelled back loud enough for everyone to hear, "YES," and ran out of the library.

I jumped to catch up with him. Our walk, which really was a gallop, took us up to a soccer field. Once on the field he began to run faster so I picked up my pace to stay along side.

"Sometimes I've believed as many as six impossible things before breakfast."

Lewis Carroll

Johnny turned to me and asked, "Can you hear it too?"

"Hear what?"

With a big smile, which insinuated that I must be dense, he said, "You know the music…" then he took a few more strides, "…in your head!"

I smiled. Yes, I was dense. "Not all of us are so lucky as to hear music clearly in our heads." Then an idea sparked, "Could you tap out the rhythms you hear with your hands on your chest so I could hear it too?"

He began to play on his body the music coursing through his veins. WOW! Bobby McFerrin, Beethoven – somebody's got to meet this kid! Maybe I wasn't so dense because now I felt I understood why he couldn't sit still. Could you sit still if symphonies were playing stereophonically in your head?

When we got back to the classroom it was computer time. Johnny and I sat at a computer. I showed Johnny where to place his fingers. I suggested he play one of his rhythms on the keypad but use the order of the letters of his name. He began to type lightning fast his full name over, over and over again. We were swimming beautifully.

Mrs. Bee was impressed with his focus. I tried to explain the magical discovery about Johnny but she was not interested. She was just pleased he was typing, not disrupting her class and doing what he was told.

When Johnny's mom came to pick him up I joyfully shared with her what I discovered and enthusiastically gave her several names of musicians in the area that could work with Johnny. My hope was that if he could get the music out and express it that we might be able to help him focus better in other areas of his life. And who knows, maybe we would benefit from the Mozart of this century? His mother was very excited.

The next morning I was called into the principal's office Fortunately, I was used to this from my own childhood school experience. It was explained to me that it was inappropriate for me to talk directly to the parent. I had breached protocol. Flash flood!

My rebuttal – my attempt to swim the torrent in the moment – was to state that when I was hired, my resume may not have been completely read. I pointed out that, right at the top, I clearly stated that my goal with children was to help them discover a more defined sense of self which in turn creates confidence, respect, understanding of boundaries and most importantly, self-love.

The principal responded by explaining how I crossed inappropriate boundaries to speak of love, and in particular, with a child like Johnny. She emphasized that it was vital not to instill false hope in a parent when we could not be sure of an outcome. She let me know that my techniques were not tried and true. Honestly, the

> *"Love shall inform your actions
> and pervade your life."*
>
> **Mahatma Gandhi**

speech was a lot longer than that but my memory plays it back as the voice of Charlie Brown's teacher in the comic *Peanuts*. Ultimately, she fired me. Sink. Sank. Sunk.

My interactions with Johnny strengthened the ideas that I had been exploring around listening for what is alive, a student's authentic presence. By observing what is truly happening for the student and validating the child's reality, I was noticing a certain quality of connection that can take place.

This type of connecting with another human being creates a mindful presence that is called empathy. Empathy is being present to what the other person is experiencing, not being stimulated by it or even trying to fix it. When we allow the person who is before us to simply be without our values, judgments or decisions placed upon them we are offering ourselves in what some have called unconditional love. Connecting to love in this way opens our heart and accesses our natural ability to respond with compassion. This loving connection engages an intrinsic motivation for the learning process. This intrinsic motivation comes alive because the teacher and the student are each connected not only to each other but also to their own authentic presence.

Discovering I was no longer there to assist her son, Johnny's mom pulled him from the school. She found a school that focused on music. He was considered a success at his new school.

When I sink in doubt I find companionship with my students. It seems that children are often in doubt...or shall we call it wonder. They are open to possibility not because they do not know better, but because they are willing to explore all options. Children want to engage with adults who are actively alive with what they are offering. Students desire the opportunity to explore learning in relationship with their teacher rather than be 'talked into' what they 'should' know about a subject. As educators, it is vital that we bring ourselves to the process of learning, fully engaging our students with our own aliveness.

This approach is different from what I was finding in the reality of being a teacher in the field of education. I found that a teacher is requested to be right; find out what is wrong with the children; to obey the administration, punish children for "bad" behavior, reward for "good" behavior; to learn all the current labels of the time to appropriately diagnose the students and to live in fear of losing their job. My early

teaching experiences stimulated great frustration in me because it seemed

that no matter the packaging of a school something about the contents in

the educational paradigm was the same.

Henry David Thoreau asked us in his essay, *On the Duty of Civil Disobedience*, "Shall we be content to obey?" I imagine that there is not one human on the planet who is content to simply obey. Yet we have educational systems in place that utilize obligation, praise, punishment, rewards, and drugs to get humans to obey. In order to obey, students disconnect from their own intrinsic motivation – their own authentic presence. In order to obey, teachers disconnect from their own intuition and creativity. This disconnection feeds an exhaustion that leads to a sense of powerlessness, hopelessness, and a fear of never being effective. The immense work that goes into simply maintaining

"The impress of your foot in the soil is felt through a thousand generations."

Daniel Quinn

these dominating educational structures where people 'obey the rules' exhausts teachers, administrators, parents, and students. What I concluded from my early teaching experiences was that there was a foundation of fear. A fear that establishes educational systems which teach classification, domination and obedience. And like Maria Montessori, I didn't want to get children to obey, I wanted to listen to my students to know how to teach. I want education to receive and empower whatever gift each being brings to this world. I want education to inspire peace.

I cordially invite you to sink and swim with me. Sink into not knowing what to do. Call into question everything you've been told about education. Even this. Immerse in your own intuition. Bathe in all your attempts to try something new, untried or even, god forbid, "not allowed".

Let's wade into discovering. Discovering our gifts, listening for our students' gifts, engaging learning as we want to engage life itself. Draw the best out of yourself, engaging the book of humanity. Sink into your doubt and swim in your ocean of creativity.

My request for you as an educator, as a human, is simple. Be curious. Be uncertain. Be puzzled.

Be undetermined.

The process of being educated has left me constipated

The American institution has not found the solution

The Student Body has lost its parts, most notably – their beating hearts

A child of five sees the world alive

To teach this being requires you seeing

How does one expect to teach by turning a child into an information leech

Overwhelmed by all the input

Their little systems shut down – KAPUT

No individualism here is inspired

Nor self-thought encouraged or acquired

Stamp them out upon the press leaving their inner worlds a mess

Oh – on the outside they look benevolent

But these duplicates are benumb and violent

They will thirst and know not what for

Implanted with low self-esteem and nothing more

A dedicated 16 years for many will pass

Never realizing they've been handed a mask

Assured time will tell we've all contributed to this living hell

BUT

What if we told little Johnny that we lied

Actually we forgot that we too, loved, laughed and cried

That everyone born eventually will die

And in between, those who desire will fly

Education is not a commodity or intelligence allowed only for the chosen piety

Numbers, letters and all things rational already live and breathe in all universal

Children are born knowing

All wisdom is discovered

In the growing

(written in 1992, inspired by Johnny)

2

⟨ℰ⟩

Mindful Heart, Heart-full Mind

*"What we are teaches the child far more than what we say, so we must be what
we want our children to become."*

Joseph Chilton Pierce

When one embarks on a radical mission it is important to take
along those who walked before you. If you were to have had the
opportunity to visit The TEMBA School you could not miss the
predominant feature upon walking in – the wall of Peace Elders. This wall
was a collection of photographs framed with wood and quotes on colored
paper of beings from all over the world who had faced great odds to teach,
live, and demonstrate nonviolence.

I spent many hours at my desk in the TEMBA library receiving
support and inspiration from these Peace Elders. As my eyes would make
contact with the thoughtful gaze of His Holiness the 14th Dali Lama, the
soulful presence of Mahatma Gandhi, the intense purposeful look of Alice

Walker, the gentle knowing of Elizabeth Kubler-Ross, the clarity of Marshall B. Rosenberg, the penetrating honesty of Dr. Martin Luther King Jr., and so many others, I would often land my gaze on the photo of a 2000-year-old redwood sequoia tree. It lived on the wall between Nelson Mandela and Mother Teresa.

This photo reminded me that, like redwoods, the students were already born with their genius intact waiting for a nourishing environment to support their growth. Students will learn to trust that no matter what life brings – strong winds that try to sway them, fiery emotions, fallen friends that can no longer grow up with them but nourish them from places unseen, or the intrusion of others who would like to cut them down, that like redwood – stored within their very cells is the wisdom for continued growth. Redwoods reminded me that although we learn the beauty of standing tall, brave and individual, it is in our foundation underneath where the nutrients for life are gathered – we hold hands, like redwood roots, with each community member.

The community we were joining hands with were indeed these elders on the wall. The presence of all these faces reminded all who walked into our school that TEMBA was building community with understanding, compassion, and a dedication to nonviolence. They offered us faith that there is the possibility to create the world we want. In fact, it is what they had devoted their lives to – a world of peace.

> *"Reflect on your decisions and ask yourself, 'Am I living the life that I want?'"*
>
> **Morris Ervin**

Peace needs to be obtained in oneself before being offered outward. One cannot create outwardly what one has not created inwardly.

Seeing the faces brought to my
attention all the individual journeys
that had taken place to elicit change in
the world. Looking into their eyes
each school day gave me support and
confidence to begin with my one

*"Those who bring sunshine
to the lives of others cannot
keep it from themselves."*

J.M. Barrie

constant source for change in the world – me. Me?! Luckily, every day at
TEMBA gave ample opportunities for learning how to attain peace
within.

Brett was one of my formidable teachers. Brett would come to
school excited to belong, ready to learn and with a smile on his face. Then
something would stimulate memory of his past. He would begin to cry,
scream and beat his fists or his head on the floor. The pain his 6-year-old
body would try to express sometimes seemed unfathomable.

TEMBA offered a safe place for Brett to heal his emotional pain
in order to give him the learning he desired. He offered me real
opportunities to take responsibility for the emotions and actions that were
directly linked to my thinking.

Brett had experiences in his infancy and early childhood where he
experienced extreme physical harm as well as being left alone for extended
periods of time with no one to respond to his needs[1]. He now lived with
his mother while his father's whereabouts were not entirely known.

We were two weeks into the school year and Brett's pain would
get triggered at some moment each day. Another teacher or I would offer

---

[1] I define needs as the energy that animates life itself. Needs, unlike preferences, wants, or
wishes, are the life force we have in common with all beings. My understanding of needs
and use of them in language is derived from Nonviolent Communication[SM] as developed
by Marshall B. Rosenberg, Ph.D.

him empathic connection while the other students continued with their class. I want to describe two consecutive days with Brett.

One day, right after morning story circle Brett's pain was stimulated. He was crying at a volume that people could hear through the walls. He was wriggling and hitting his fists against the floor. I thought, "Poor kid is not getting enough time to heal. He is trying so hard." I held him and spoke with him until his release was complete for that moment. This took about 5 minutes and then he got up to move onto his next class. I patted myself on the back with the thought that I had the patience of Mother Teresa.

The next day Brett's pain was stimulated on the way to morning circle. He dropped to the floor crying and beating fists in the classroom next to the hall where I was passing through on my own way to circle. I thought, "What a brat – why can't he just stop" and "Why do I always end up with these kinds of kids?" I responded with silent but 'audible' frustration – not saying a word and not moving toward him.

He got louder.

Finally I said, "I need a moment to myself." I didn't actually say the words as much as throw them at him in my own fit of anger.

I stepped into the doorway away from Brett, who was still screaming and crying in the classroom, not shrinking back in volume or expression. My thinking continued, "What a crappy teacher I am. I should be more compassionate." I began to self-empathize to create peace within so I could have more compassion to offer Brett. I had been up late the night before in a discussion and was stressed about personal matters. I was feeling fatigue and irritated because I needed understanding related to a personal discussion from the night before. I was also needing a little space in the moment to take time to integrate myself into the school day.

Moving from blaming myself and Brett to acknowledging my feelings and needs, I became more present and available to face the situation.

I stepped back into the classroom where Brett was now a smatter of tears and screams. I moved closer to him as I said, "Brett, I see how much support you need right now. I have had so little sleep and have such worry about things that have nothing to do with you. I feel afraid all I can offer now is impatience and frustration." Meanwhile he is still crying and pounding the floor. "I would like to hold you and give you what you need but in this moment I need some space to care for what is happening inside of me. Could you wait until lunch and we can share that time together?" He stopped his fist mid-strike to the floor. The tears stopped. He stood up and said, "I would be willing Catherine," and went off to morning circle. Can you just imagine how far my jaw dropped in that moment?

We did share lunch that day and he did offer his tears up again. I noticed with Brett, as I have with other students, that teachers including me had a challenging time with him if they saw only the fixed ideas they projected on him, whether it was positive or negative. From those two consecutive days with Brett, I realized that my biggest obstacle in connecting with my students, or giving in the way I would like is my own thinking. How I perceive someone or a situation influences how I respond.

"The most beautiful things in the world cannot be seen or even touched, they must be felt with the heart."

Helen Keller

As educators, not only are we trained to create fixed ideas, diagnoses, and judgments, we are told to write them down and pass them along with each student as an assessment of who that human is and how one 'should' interact with them. Brett's file was no exception and was quite filled with what others thought of him and who they believed him to be. It has been my experience that diagnosing to assess or "case filing" has not been an effective long-term strategy for changing choices in behavior or supporting a child to become a life-long learner. Labeling in this way actually can block our ability to connect empathically and build the quality of relationship we would like with our students.

The first step to building my relationship with my students is to be clear on my intention in each moment of interaction. My intention is: *I want to connect.* Contrary to my training in the teacher credential program, I do not actually have the ability to control or to "get my way." Recently in a training I was offering, two teens and a nine year old were in the crowd. When I was explaining the point I am touching on here, adding, "It's almost as if kids can smell when adults want to 'get their way'," all three nodded "yes".

It is a very slippery slope to "want my way." If for one moment I believe that I can get my way, get control over the situation, or even think I can change the behavior of another, I will lose all opportunity for real connection and trust. If I believe I have to get my way, then I have denied choice to all, including myself, in the situation. I will begin to act or speak based on the evaluations and judgments I have about the student or myself perpetuating a dynamic of "power over"/ "power under."

> *"Loving kindness is the wish to see others enjoy happiness"*
>
> **His Holiness the 14th Dalai Lama**

Going back to that first day with Brett, if my intention had been to "get my way," even if "my way" was for him to heal his pain, then by

46

trying to control or manipulate his behavior, I would have established "power over" him. His response would have been like so many other students I have met when they are approached by someone trying to influence "power over' them, he would have rebelled. Brett's particular rebellion would have looked like moving from his own personal tantrum to acting it out by trying to beat up another kid. Under the training I had originally as a teacher I would then have had to give a punishment of some kind to get him to comply with what I wanted. As I write this, I am remembering how exhausting it was to work in this way.

If I had approached Brett on the second day with the intention to "get my way", which in that moment was to be left alone, I would have been creating a "power under" situation. Believing that Brett had the most power due to his expression of pain, I would have proceeded with the illusion of having no power, giving rise to two choices: blame him or blame myself. Blame often arises when we believe we have no power or choice in a situation. When this occurs we invite in our own rebellion. In my situation with Brett my rebellion would have looked like ignoring him, not expressing myself, and not enjoying my day. I can recall far too many times like that in my early days of teaching, where my rebellious behavior was actively disconnecting me from my students and my passion for teaching.

> *"Freedom is the ability to pause between stimulus and response. And in the pause choose."*
>
> **Rollo May**

Intention, by definition, is a determination to act in a specified way. I want my actions, even my words, to reflect my determination to connect. So, this first step I take in each moment intending to connect acknowledges the choice that is really there in each given situation. When

I acknowledge that I and others have choice at every moment, I help to create "power with" my students. This means that I no longer spend the day in the classroom trying to control other people's behaviors. I get to do what I came there to do, learn with my students.

I never read Brett's file, or any other student's file that transferred to TEMBA. If I am to maintain an intention of connection I want to meet the human in front of me, fresh each moment. I want the authentic presence of each student to have a chance to express, be seen, and be understood without pre-judgments or evaluations.

Gandhi wrote, "True education must correspond to the surrounding circumstances or it is not a healthy growth." If I act from my fixed ideas, intending to get my way, I am not authentically present to the surrounding circumstances, the present moment. Transforming our fixed ideas, diagnoses and judgments of ourselves and of others creates a heart-full mind. This mind takes time to observe what is happening without projecting fixed ideas or being attached to assessing it one way or the other. This heart-full mind observes in order to connect to what is happening with our own and others' authentic presence.

We have been educated to believe that the mind is logical and the heart is emotional. I believe they are linked and share both qualities. The word emotion comes from a Latin root of *emovere*. When translated, *emovere* actually means 'to set the mind in motion'. When we set our mind into motion with just thoughts and fixed ideas, without connection to the heart's listening, then we run the risk of choosing actions that are

> *"Many great sorrows of the world arise when the mind is disconnected from the heart."*
>
> **Jack Kornfield**

ineffective and create disconnection. Each moment is an experiment with becoming more and more present to the person we are becoming, thereby allowing us to become more and more present with the person with whom we wish to connect.

When we connect the mind with the heart and transcend our fixed ideas about people or situations we change our quality of listening from selective to empathic. We no longer hear only what will reinforce our judgments or fixed ideas, we become aware of the human needs that are alive in us and in others. This quality of listening increases our presence to allow us to see the individual as they are in the present moment. Engaging the present moment in this way increases the empathic connection between people.

My guess, based on Brett's feedback, is that he could sense my intention was to connect with him, not make him stop his behavior. He could feel my presence, the kind of presence that gave him space to self-connect. Returning to his own authentic presence, rather than looking outside of himself for something to heal or fix him, he connected to his own need to be understood. He also had a desire to contribute to me. His willingness to get to class was essentially his own clarity that he would later get the presence and focus he truly wanted. When we open to the vulnerability of the moment with what is alive in us, our authentic presence, our human needs, we build understanding and trust in the connection with our students.

Sixteen-year-old Zeke was an active member of the Ku Klux Klan. I had the opportunity to work in high schools in the San Francisco Bay Area teaching nonviolence in a two-day workshop format. The first day was spent working on exactly what we have been discussing in this chapter: how to transcend our thinking, fixed ideas and our perceptions of others while connecting to human needs. The second day, we supported connection between students in the class as well as empowered them with conflict resolution skills.

By the second day Zeke had sat with his discomfort in a room with people he saw as Jewish, Gay, Black, Liberal, the wrong kind of White, and Female until he could no longer keep quiet. During a game, when it was a revealed that a Jewish girl's older sister would be having a wedding ceremony the following summer to marry another woman, he did not hesitate to voice out loud what was happening in his mind, "That's just wrong!"

"Are you uncomfortable because there are people in here you are not used to connecting with?" I asked.

Zeke replied with reasoning to explain his beliefs about why certain people are just "born inferior". After a monologue that stimulated agitation in several people throughout the room, he added, "Well, you know I hate these people. Don't get me wrong. I'm not a violent person. I wouldn't want harm to come to them. It's just I hate certain people."

"Well, now I'm confused because you're saying you hate these people yet you don't want any harm to come to them. I am guessing you might even have some confusion about your feelings towards these people because you say you don't want to be violent yet you speak of hate." Zeke continued to listen

> *" Labels block compassion."*
>
> **Marshall B. Rosenberg, Ph.D.**

with his arms folded across his chest, his eyes fixed on mine. "I'm still confused about your choice to be a member of the KKK. From what I've known they have created an amazing amount of violence against the folks you say you hate. Can you tell me why you joined? What was your primary motivation to join?"

Zeke looked right into me, "My dad is a member of the KKK!"

The room bristled with comments. One student, Terrance, chimed in, "Ah man, just cause your dad's a hater doesn't mean you gotta be one too!"

Nodding to that profound statement, I added, looking as intensely into Zeke's eyes as he had into mine, "I'm actually hearing how much you'd like to connect to your dad. I am also hearing that maybe you feel conflicted about being a member of an organization that tries to create connection through violence and hating others." Leaning toward Zeke, trying to tangibly soften the room with my presence, "Has this really met your need to connect with your father?"

Zeke's eyes swelled with water but he was not going to cry, not in front of this group. "Yeah," Zeke paused to take a full inhale and exhale audible to the room, maybe a bit from the gravity of the realization and a bit to stop the tears. "I guess I joined cuz I wanted to connect to my dad. I just wanna get along with him."

When Zeke sat in an empathic connection that could afford him the opportunity to connect his own mind and heart, he realized that he had not joined the KKK because he hated certain people but rather, he was desperate to find a way to connect with his father.

"As we are liberated from fear, our presence automatically liberates others."

Marianne Williamson

He walked up to me after the workshop, "You know, that was the first time I felt fear begin to leave my body. I'm actually relieved."

With his new clarity he began to assess the effectiveness of his choice and decided that hating others was not truly his path, not an expression of his authentic presence. He was able to get past the enemy images his mind had created and the fixed ideas he had about himself to see what he needed. Zeke quit the KKK, developed all sorts of friends, and continued to work on various strategies to find connection with his dad.

We, humans, are in constant motion to meet our needs. What strategies we choose will be defined by how connected we are to the needs that motivate that choice. Engaging the heart by developing a quality of listening that can identify needs creates a mindful presence in our ability to connect. The mindful heart clarifies the human needs that are alive in the moment. With clarity of what is truly needed for the being to thrive, the heart then connects to the mind for solution.

The mind wants to offer possible solutions each moment we engage it. Ondrea Levine describes the mind this way, "There is a pie and your mind says, 'Go ahead, have some.' Then after eating the pie, your mind says, 'I wouldn't have done that if I were you.' And this is the mind to whom we go for advice?" If we engage our mind without the listening of the heart we run the risk of making choices based on our evaluations about the person. The heart's listening for human needs dissolves the judgments, restoring the opportunity to connect and create understanding.

> *"it is only with the heart that one can see rightly, what is essential is invisible to the eye."*
>
> **Antoine de Saint-Exupery**

Education is about relationships. Creating empathic connections and non-judgmental learning environments, we support integrating emotional pain so learners can learn. With clarity of intention to connect, an authentic presence, and a focus on the human needs that are alive, we establish an empathic connection with our students. This allows a self-full awareness to develop in learners which inspires them to make effective choices to meet their own needs as well as others' needs. Their decisions become life-serving, allowing us to access the endless possibilities of learning.

If I can internalize what I wish to see in my classroom then I begin to contribute to peace, ease, and learning for my students and for me. My mentor, Gloria Cooper, once said to me, "When you teach, you bring a field of energy – the field is of your choosing." When I looked within and asked myself what would I enjoy my field to be, I decided I wanted it to be as Rumi describes in his poem:

> *Out beyond ideas of wrongdoing and rightdoing,*
> *there is a field. I'll meet you there.*

With both Brett and Zeke, I did not see them as wrong for their behaviors or beliefs. I saw humans expressing themselves. By seeing them as human, I was able to engage the heart's mindfulness of listening and the mind's heart-full ability to find solution, allowing me to meet them in Rumi's field. If I want my students to respond compassionately, take responsibility for their words and behaviors, and make life-serving decisions so they can reach their fullest potential as learners, then that is exactly what I must do.

I have learned that the most valuable tool I can bring into the classroom is **LOVE**. Each day, having set my intention for connection and brought my full authentic presence to the moment, I **Listen** for the human needs that are alive in each word or action, **Observe** what is actually happening in the given moment and **Validate** it as true for each individual's experience, and **Empathize** to create a quality of connection that builds trust, understanding, and alliances for learning.

> *When the soul lies down in that grass,*
> *the world is too full to talk about.*
> *Ideas, language, even the phrase each other,*
> *doesn't make any sense.*

3

The Three R's

"Everything the power of the world does is done in a circle."

Black Elk

Take a moment right now to imagine your perfect life. Really, take a moment now to breathe. Allow a full breath in and then out. Rest into the place where you are reading this book and feel your own sense of being alive. Listen to your heart beating. Now imagine. Imagine your perfect life. What would your life be like if everything you ever wished for came to pass? Observe, who is in this perfect life of yours. What are you and these people doing, how are you interacting in this life together? Give texture, color, and sound to your imagined life. Validate any possibility you imagine. Give yourself the opportunity to bring forth any vision of how you'd enjoy living your life. Resting deeper into this vision, Empathize. What is the essence of this life you've imagined? What words describe the qualities present in your unique vision? Take a moment and write a few of these words down.

I have offered this exercise of "Imagine Your Perfect Life" to hundreds of people, on six different continents, and found that we humans really want the same qualities in life, regardless of culture or age. If you had seen the list of qualities that came from the 41 children in Kabul, Afghanistan, or the sixth grade class in McGregor, South Africa, or the 55 educators in Australia that did this same exercise you likely would have noticed similarities to your list. Did you happen to write down respect, health, rest, ease, freedom, choice, love, trust, safety, protection, play, to be understood, connection, humor, or creativity? If you did, then you can see your common humanity, even with people in cultures or countries different from yours. These words that you have discovered to name the quality of life you would enjoy living are human needs, the qualities of our one life together, our common humanity. If listening, observing, validating, and empathizing are the bricks of our foundation for peace and nonviolence, then naming, understanding, and connecting to human needs is the raw material, which forges the bricks. Living this practice of LOVE becomes the mortar to hold it all together.

By listening for human needs within ourselves in each moment and choosing the actions that would most serve the life we want, we Respect Self. The first of the 3 R's we practiced at TEMBA, Respect Self invites us to self-connect and self-empathize. When we break respect down to its Latin roots of "re" and "spect" we find a deeper meaning of the word. "Re" means "again". "Spect" means "to look". An underlying meaning of respect is "to look again". When we self-empathize, we take a moment to look again, past our surface thoughts, and bring awareness to the universal human needs inside. These needs are alive all the time, in any circumstance, but can hard to recognize when we're stimulated.

The second of the three R's is Respect Other. In order to create the "power-with" dynamic – building safety, trust, respect, and understanding in the school community, we also want to be willing "to look again" when someone did not behave in a way we enjoyed or things did not go the way we hoped. By observing what is, validating one another's experience in terms of the commonality of needs, and empathizing, we are able to actively Respect Other, simply with our willingness "to look again."

When people would hear of TEMBA and its foundation in peace and nonviolence, an assumption was often made that there should never be any conflicts or somehow we could magically avoid them. Actually, we developed an understanding of the nature of conflict and the quality of connection that could arise between people if the interactions were met with listening, observing, validating, and empathizing. Veritably, we didn't

> *"Peace is not the absence of conflict, but the presence of creative alternatives for responding to conflict."*
>
> **Dorothy Thompson**

see conflicts, we saw opportunities to Respect Self and Other, to look again at the interaction so we could build trusting relationships for learning.

In "power over" educational structures, conflict is seen as an obstacle to be removed. These structures put into place some authority to be 'in power' to remove the obstacle and end the conflict. This inevitably creates more conflict because we are putting into place only one strategy – the teacher or principal. I enjoy the definition of conflict that Sura Hart and Victoria Kindle Hodson give in their book *The Compassionate Classroom*:

> Conflicts occur when we think that there is only one way or one
> person to meet a need. Conflicts also occur when the strategy

chosen to meet a need means that some other important needs will not get met – mine or yours.

In a "power-with" educational structure we no longer play this game where teacher or principal have absolute authority to solve problems and resolve conflicts. Instead, teachers' "authority" is related to their body of experience. At TEMBA, we clarified this at the start of each school year through what we called an "Honoring Ceremony".

Within the first days of school, teachers and students would stand together in a circle. The power of the circle is in its shape. When people stand in a circle, they can see every other person with ease, initiating true equality. I would share with the group that we all have inhabited our bodies for different lengths of time. This length of time does not necessarily equate to how much knowledge one has but rather what kind of knowledge one has based on their set of experiences. I would share that we were all here to create a community to learn from one another. Then we each took a turn to present our age, our body of experience, to the group.

We use wording from indigenous North American people's tradition. The presenter says, "I have walked the Earth for (age) years." Then the group responds with, "It will be an honor to walk with you this coming year." Everyone bows as a physical expression of honor. Then the next presenter takes his or her turn. By the end of the ceremony we have validated our differences and honored our equal footing as humans, ready to embark on the chaotic journey of learning together, as community.

Establishing our learning community in this way clarifies that the people in the school who walk in the role of teachers have years of experience surpassing the people who walk in the role of students. Hence, the teachers will offer guidance on various subjects, but in no way hold "power over" other individuals. Utilizing the "Honoring Ceremony" introduces the teachers' and students' unique body of experiences allowing the onset of a "power-with" structure for the school year. Regardless of roles, age, or life experiences, all people are equally human and share a responsibility to the learning community. This acknowledgment of differences and recognition of responsibility asks each of us to learn, practice, and live the skills of listening, observing, validating, and empathizing. We engage a trust that all needs can be met, that all beings can thrive.

Now, discerning our needs from our strategies can be quite a challenge. We can confuse our preferences of how we would enjoy our needs to be met for the actual need that is trying to be expressed. I'd like to clarify by sharing part of a discussion from a class of mine from a South San Francisco high school.

I asked, "What do humans need?" As the answers flew verbally at me, I wrote them in no particular order on the chalkboard, only distinguishing them into two untitled lists. *(see Figure 1, next page)*

Then I asked them to look at the words they answered and tell me the difference between the two lists. One girl answered, "We can live without the list on the right but we can't live without the one on the left." Another student jumped in, "Yeah, one list is what you really need and the other is what you want!"

One boy continued to explain, "The list on the right, yeah that one, we can live without that stuff, even though I'd really like to keep a few," he chuckled a bit, "but, that list, the one on the left, man, that's life!"

When we lay it out on paper, or in this case the chalkboard, we can start to see with some ease the difference between the quality with

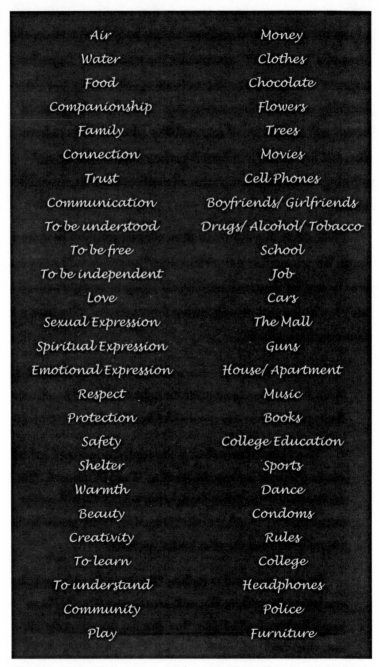

Air	Money
Water	Clothes
Food	Chocolate
Companionship	Flowers
Family	Trees
Connection	Movies
Trust	Cell Phones
Communication	Boyfriends/ Girlfriends
To be understood	Drugs/ Alcohol/ Tobacco
To be free	School
To be independent	Job
Love	Cars
Sexual Expression	The Mall
Spiritual Expression	Guns
Emotional Expression	House/ Apartment
Respect	Music
Protection	Books
Safety	College Education
Shelter	Sports
Warmth	Dance
Beauty	Condoms
Creativity	Rules
To learn	College
To understand	Headphones
Community	Police
Play	Furniture

Figure 1 – "What do humans need?" from a South San Francisco High School.
Needs were listed on the left, Strategies on the right.

which we would like to live our lives and the things we bring into our life to enrich those qualities. We can distinguish the difference between our authentic human needs and the strategies or preferences to meet those needs.

Then the question arises – how do we really know what we need? How do we figure out what is alive in us so that we can clearly assess what strategy would be most effective for getting our needs and other's needs met?

One student came up with the following idea. He brought forth that our feelings were like indicator lights on the dashboard of a car. Our needs are the fluids necessary for the car to run. Indicator lights let us know how our fluids our doing. Our feelings let us know how our needs our doing. We can use our feelings to connect to our needs. I like this metaphor because it takes all the right/wrong ideas off of emotions. There are no good or bad feelings, simply indicators of what is alive in us, what we might need in any particular moment. Biologically, emotions last about nine seconds. That is the amount of time it takes for cerebral fluid to travel the spine and wash over the brain. This is the root of the "count to ten" anger management tool. Counting to ten does allow for the cerebral fluid to flow and wash over for an emotional shift but the risk can be that it can go from anger to rage not necessarily anger to calm. I believe pausing is a valuable idea, but I'd like to be clear what we'd like to do in that pause.

> *"Only learn to take our anger and our hate, control our mental state, settle down and just set it straight, maybe we can learn to take a second to pump the brakes 'for we said it, regret it later, and let it escalate!"*
>
> **TuPac Shakur**

When we pause after realizing we are stimulated, it gives us a moment to look again, to contact the needs that are alive in us. If we have the awareness that our emotions become stimulated to indicate what need is alive in us then we can take responsibility for our feelings, thoughts, and actions. Responsibility to our thoughts, feelings, needs, and actions is the third of the fundamental R's when educating with a foundation in nonviolence. In order to enact this kind of responsibility we practice listening, observing, validating, and empathizing. We become the mortar for a foundation in peace and nonviolence.

In a private school in Buenos Aires, Argentina where I offered training for educators, I had the joy to play with some of the students in the classroom. The director of the school wanted me to start with the class that was having the "hardest" time with conflicts because "the bully" of the school was in this classroom. She was just about to say one more thing to reveal whom they thought of as "the bully" of the school. I asked not to be told anything more, but rather if they still felt they would like me to know I could make a guess after the class.

The director walked me into a classroom where a teacher was leading the students in a discussion on feelings, how others make us feel certain ways, and how we must control our behavior to not upset others so we can stop conflict. I sat for a moment in an empty student's chair to listen. I began to tell myself all sorts of things evaluating and judging what I was witnessing. Practicing the first of TEMBA's 3 R's, I looked again at what was happening within me. Observing the thought, "she's educating children to blame others for their feelings", I realized that telling myself this stimulated feelings of worry and concern. These feelings let me know that I need clarity for what I believe and contribution to peaceful relationships. By taking the time to Respect Self in this way, I was then able to Respect Other, appreciating that the teacher I was evaluating probably also wanted clarity and contribution to peaceful relationships. Taking Responsibility for my thoughts, feelings, and needs, I opened my mouth and offered, "Could I ask a question?"

The teacher invited me to come up to the chalkboard. I asked, "Where do feelings actually come from?" Several students raised their hands.

One student replied, "Su mente! Your mind."

Another, "El Cuerpo! The body."

Another, "Su corazón! Your heart."

I began to feel relief and said, "I am so excited to hear these responses because I agree that feelings come from within us. I do not believe someone else causes them."

With an expression of confusion, the teacher asked, "Could you explain more please?"

"I see feelings as wonderful indicators to let me know the needs that are alive in me. But first, let's clarify a need. What do humans need?" Then we played the list game to reveal needs and strategies.

Realizing that our feelings indicate the needs alive in us, we can take responsibility not only for those emotions, but for the thoughts and actions we choose. If we pause for a moment when an emotion arises to assess the needs then our thinking shifts into responsibility, which reveals doable effective actions to serve those needs. If we can clearly identify the needs that are alive in us moment to moment then we can begin to clearly discern the strategies that will be most effective. So when the students in the Buenos Aires classroom began to play with needs they immediately identified the needs for safety, trust, and respect as being the most important for them as a group. We played a couple more games to determine the strategies this class would like to use to meet those needs.

After the class, the teacher came up to me with tears in her eyes, "You know I was telling the kids what I had been told all my life, that I was the cause of other people's pain. This, this was really freeing."

The school director joined us, "I am very curious if you could tell who "the bully" was, because he did not do one thing he usually does!"

I named a student, one who had participated with exuberant aliveness, answering questions, and fully engaged from start to finish. The director and teacher both nodded "yes". With shock on her face, the director asked, "How could you tell?"

"It has been my experience that the ones we label 'bully' are students expressing their unmet needs quite tragically. They are in need of empathy. When that empathy becomes available to them, they respond with exuberant life and willing connection. I am also guessing today's class had a lot of meaning for him because he felt delighted to be fully included in the process of deciding what would contribute to safety, trust, and respect in the classroom." My interactions with him included him, simply by listening to him as I would any other student and validating his presence with empathic connection.

"We don't make it, until we all make it."

Mahatma Gandhi

When we invite ourselves, and our students, to take responsibility and be part of the group, engaging the authentic presence alive in each one of us, we establish our foundation in nonviolence, giving the connection needed for learning. The "Honoring Ceremony" that TEMBA does at the beginning of each year initiates belonging for all, asking each person to take responsibility. Acknowledging the need to belong and requesting that all take responsibility builds the "power-with" structure within the classroom. We bring into practice a world that includes everyone, with the potential for thriving in peace.

TEMBA fostered the three R's by cultivating opportunities to train in listening with a Mindful Heart, observing with a Heart-full Mind, validating one another's presence, and empathizing. We increased the space between stimulus and response in any given interaction so we could practice compassion, equanimity and conciliatory behaviors. Gandhi referred to this examining of interactions and human relations as "experiments in truth." With a "power-with" dynamic in the TEMBA classroom, we received each interaction as an experiment in truth. At times, we would slow the practice down to expand understanding and increase connection. TEMBA called these particular experiments – Circles.

> *"True education flowers at the point when delight falls in love with responsibility."*
>
> **Philip Pullman**

A Circle is a dialogue to restore connection, understanding, and trust among two or more people. If a person is having a conflict or wants support in an interaction they call for a Circle. A Circle consists of the people wanting connection and understanding restored, anyone who was affected by whatever it was that took place, and a facilitator. Each person in the Circle engages the 3 R's: Respect Self, Respect Other, and Responsibility for their own thoughts, feelings, needs, and actions. When empathic connection and mutual understanding is gained then effective strategies can be brought forth to meet the needs named during the Circle dialogue.

The facilitator can, at times, be the most challenging role, for they do not rule, decide, or judge. Most conflict resolution models allow the facilitator "power-over" the group by having the facilitator determine the best course of action or who-hurt-who more. In a "power-with" Circle, the facilitator is an equal member on the Circle, essentially being a "third-sider" to the situation. Being a "third-sider" means being on the side of peace or on the side of restoring connection. The "third-sider", or facilitator in TEMBA terms, offers support for empathic connection. They care for the bringing forward of needs that want to be expressed by all in the Circle.

> *"Harmony comes from the reconciliation of opposites by a third element, bringing them all to a new unity."*
>
> **Michael S. Schneider**

I must confess that having everyone, including students, participate in the role of facilitator in a Circle did not actually begin until the last two months of the first year of TEMBA. I had slipped back into, without even realizing how habitual it was, the old belief that the teacher is the one strategy to help resolve conflict in the classroom.

Although we witnessed many conflicts resolved in a wonderfully new way, what developed was that Circles began to be threats: "I'm gonna call a Circle on you!" I was aghast to say the least. I so wanted resolution to happen peaceably without any hierarchy or punishment that I had not seen the subtle violence of what we were creating.

In my confusion and utter dismay of why circles were turning into threats, I called my friend who was a Center for Nonviolent Communication Certified Trainer[2], Julie Greene. Julie supported my

---

[2] The Center for Nonviolent Communication[SM] has a certification process for people interested in working within its global network of trainers. (www.cnvc.org)

efforts with the school by giving me empathic connection around what ever was troubling me, and offering trainings for the parents. In response to my call, she said Marshall Rosenberg, the founder of Nonviolent Communication^{SM} was in town and invited me to come talk with her and Marshall. I told them about the Circle process TEMBA was using. I let them know that at the beginning of the year Circles went quite well and seemed to offer a whole new way of solving all kinds of disagreements. But in recent months we were encountering students who were using Circles as threats, "I'm gonna call a Circle on you." I expressed how it felt like the same energy as the old fashioned threat I heard all too often in schools where I worked, "I'm gonna tell on you!"

Marshall asked me, "Who do you have facilitating these circles?"

I explained, "The teachers are the facilitators, but I don't understand the problem because they all took trainings in Nonviolent Communication, including several who trained directly with you."

"If the person you are talking to doesn't appear to be listening, be patient. It may simply be that he has a small piece of fluff in his ear."

Winnie the Pooh

He smiled. He said, "You still have an authority figure."

Julie and Marshall both agreed that training everyone, including the students, to be facilitators releases any one person from having authority, and thus the threat would lose its power. TEMBA immediately implemented this idea.

TEMBA kids were always very excited to share with new kids that their school had no principal. Often that was the first thing explained to them on the playground. "REALLY! We have no principal! You don't get in trouble here, but you got to take responsibility for all your thoughts, feelings, and actions." I would say the Circle process was not so much formally taught as simply passed on, because kids liked to watch Circles even when they didn't involve them directly. I am guessing that it contributed to learning as well as enjoyment to witness compassionate action.

Circles can happen anytime. Sometimes they happen immediately after conflict arises or sometimes a Circle is formed after class. If I'm not asked to be part of a Circle, I will continue teaching and the students can find a place within the classroom to have their Circle. If the Circle involves me in any way, and I understand that it serves my needs as well as others, then I pause the class

> *"When we focus on clarifying what is being observed, felt, and needed rather than diagnosing or judging, we discover the depth of our own compassion."*
>
> **Marshall B. Rosenberg, Ph.D.**

and participate. If I am connected to needs that would not be served by me pausing class then I request that the Circle happen after class. When a Circle takes place during class time, then students who are not involved in the Circle sometimes stop what they are doing to bear witness.

The following is a real circle that took place during lunchtime with two students: Al, age six, and Frank, age seven. I was the facilitator. The students had been in school together at TEMBA for one month.

AL: He hit me with a block.

FRANK: I did not.

FACILITATOR: Hold on. Can we try that again without assuming anyone is to blame?

AL: I was building my tower when a block hit me in the head.

FRANK: I was running through here minding my own business.

FACILITATOR: Frank, I hear you were running through here. What were your actual actions not your defense of them?

FRANK: I was running through here trying to dribble these blocks pretending they were basketballs.

FACILITATOR: Thank you. Now that we can see what happened let's look at what feelings got stimulated and the needs behind them. O.K. Al, what feeling was stimulated when the block hit your head?

AL: It hurt my head and I got sad and really mad. He shouldn't run and…

FACILITATOR: Hold on. We will make requests in a moment. Let's take it one step at a time. I am hearing you were feeling sad and mad so I'm guessing you might want safety while you're playing. Is that true?

AL: Yeah. I want my body safe.

FACILITATOR: Thank you. Frank, curious what feelings were stimulated when you were running and dribbling pretend basketballs?

FRANK: I was really happy… just playing.

FACILITATOR: Feeling happy because I'm guessing your need for play was really alive. Is that what was true for you?

FRANK: Yeah.

FACILITATOR: O.K. let's take a moment and see if we heard each other. Al, will you let Frank know what you heard his feelings and needs to be?

AL: Yeah, you were really happy because you wanted to play.

FACILITATOR: And Frank will you let Al know what you heard his feelings and needs to be?

FRANK: You said you felt scared because you want to know you won't get hit with a block.

FACILITATOR: Does that meet your need for understanding Al?

AL: Yeah, I was scared too. I just want to be safe.

FACILITATOR: I am guessing you would really like to trust you are safe when you play blocks.

FRANK: You want to be safe and you would like me to help protect you? (He said this with a big smile on his face.)

FACILITATOR: I'm guessing we are ready for requests. What would the two of you like to support the needs of safety and play?

FRANK: Would you like to play pretend basketball with me?

AL: No, I just want to build. Would you not run with the blocks for the rest of lunch?

FRANK: But I want to play with the blocks my way. What if I played with them over there away from your building area?

AL: That would work for me. You can come build if you want.

Incidentally, after Frank played pretend basketball for quite awhile he went over and began building with Al. Circles offer resolution for conflicts in the moment and help build trusting relationships. The very fact that people sit and listen to one another, to really hear each other's human needs, encourages meaningful friendships.

Because the dialogue in a Circle is to establish empathic connection, it does not require knowing details. In the situation with Al and Frank, I helped with translating their words into needs. Notice that I did not spend any time asking what happened or why a block hit the boy, nor did I imply blame or wrongness in any way. Details are only desired if there is to be a judgment of right or wrong. I offered support for connection and tried to really see the human needs that were being spoken. I trusted that if my guesses were not accurate they would have let me know. Notice how the boys were able to return to an authentic connection. The connection was merely identified and given a moment to be, then life continued with new strategies for action in place.

My greatest joy every school year is watching the transformation of formal Circles with facilitators turn into informal Circle dialogues. The power of using the formal Circle allows the three R's to develop. Everyone gets the chance to build skills of empathic listening and expressing of needs. Our Circles are formal practices with empathic

"Sometimes, I do lose sight of compassion but I never feel more satisfied than when I resolve an argument the way I was taught at TEMBA - with open ears and an open heart."

Hannah Muller, 17

connection so that we can begin to respond compassionately in our daily interactions. Connecting to needs with an ability to dialogue about them, we can begin to ask community members how we can contribute to one another.

There were plenty of times we slipped back into our habits of "wanting to get our way" rather than engaging the willingness to connect. When this happened we noticed immediately because life would become un-fun. We would find ourselves not enjoying interactions and returning to habitual responses of obligation, duty, guilt, fear, and blame. When people respond to each other in this energy, they do not get the wonderful opportunity to access their own natural giving. We miss the chance to connect.

As a teacher I walk with two questions that Marshall Rosenberg gave me once in training. The two questions he offered had to do with avoiding violence and accessing this natural giving: What do I want the person to do differently? What do I want the other person's reasons to be

71

to do what I want them to do? I found these questions invaluable in keeping me honest about whether I wanted "to get my way" or I wanted to authentically connect, especially in the case of class work or homework,

"It is not how much we do, it is how much love we put in the doing."

Mother Teresa

where I could sometimes convince myself that I was "right" in "wanting my way" and children "should" do their work. I would remind myself that if a student completes their homework only because their teacher "says so", then they are simply learning to obey authority, without engaging their intrinsic motivation for learning. The following is an actual Circle I had with a student at TEMBA:

> FACILITATOR: O.K. who called the circle, will you begin with what happened?
>
> CATHERINE: For three days she has not brought in her homework. Ugh, this is really hard. I have so many judgments in my mind– I can't get past them.
>
> FACILITATOR: O.K. Catherine, why don't you just speak sloppy and I'll help you translate. Sara, you can cover your ears unless you think you can listen without taking it personally.
>
> CATHERINE: She is such a prepubescent brat with such a snobby attitude. I can't take here attitude anymore. I am so angry I can't even look at her.
>
> FACILITATOR: Sounds to me, Catherine, like you're really upset and concerned about Sara's safety and well-being. Also, you'd like to have your needs for respect and cooperation met.
>
> CATHERINE: (beginning to cry) Yes! (looking to Sara) I just want to know you are O.K. and when I see that your work is not being done I feel worried and I want to offer support and I'm feeling confused about how.

SARA: (now crying too) I want to respect you and I want to do my work but I have just felt so confused lately. So many things are changing for me.

The facilitator was Eve. She was nine-years-old at the time of this Circle. She offered me freedom of expression without labeling it as right or wrong while simultaneously offering protection to the other person. Her translation was incredibly helpful in clarifying what was really happening for me. Her translation helped open all the hearts in the Circle.

The conversation continued to reveal some of the things that were happening at home for Sara and how she would like my support. I was able to request the manner in which I would enjoy receiving her homework. For the last four months of school, her work was not late and she spoke to me when she needed support.

This Circle afforded me the opportunity to transcend my thoughts about my student and make an authentic connection. I really

"Freedom is not worth having if it does not include the freedom to make mistakes."

Mahatma Gandhi

appreciated how the facilitator handled my enemy image thinking. It help me shift from me "wanting to get my way", getting her homework to me, to making an empathic connection. This Circle helped to build a trusting relationship that still exists today. Sara emailed just a couple months ago to share about the college she is attending. It is in these precious moments that we take pause, to listen and empathize, to shift how we think and respond, that can make an impact for life.

Contrary to what you might be imagining at this point in reading about these Circles, they do not take all day or take the place of academic learning. In fact, the academic learning is enhanced because when students know they belong and the classroom is held in safety, trust, and respect they enter learning through their inherent choosing. It is true that some Circles last longer than others, and some lasted longer than I enjoyed, but the students I have seen move from TEMBA out into the world embrace learning as a life-long creative process. Indeed, they leave knowing all interactions become experiments in truth and a chance to practice the three R's: Respect Self, Respect Others, and Responsibility for all actions.

By the way, I did take a long look at the traditional three R's in education. Did anyone ever notice that those three R's: Reading, Writing, and Arithmetic, actually don't all begin with R, and in fact, were we to play with their beginning letters, we could possibly have an acronym for WAR? It became very clear to me that the 3 R's: Respect Self, Respect Others, and Responsibility for all actions[3] more reliably engage learners in a way that establishes a foundation in peace and nonviolence. When we are aware of this power of choice in our actions we access an intrinsic motivation and become authentically engaged in the processes of learning. We become aware that we create each moment's possibility of peace or conflict. Writing, arithmetic, and reading then become strategies in which we can express our authentic presence, meet human needs, and interact with the world around us.

At every moment, children are developing their ability to decide how to best meet their own needs, including how meeting their needs affects meeting the needs of others. In the practice of listening, observing, validating, and empathizing we can reflect on how to find a strategy to meet all needs. My hope is that each child will look within,

---

[3] I first found The 3 R's: Respect Self, Respect Others, and Responsibility for all actions in H. Jackson Brown, Jr.'s *Life's Little Instruction Book*.

and assess if their needs will truly be met by the chosen strategy. I want children, actually all of us, to access natural giving. I trust that if people are given at least one opportunity to return to an empathic connection, it is stored in their memory and they can return to it again and again. Every interaction is a chance to build a foundation in peace and nonviolence. Every moment is a moment to engage learning.

4

❧

Order Out of Chaos

"If the world is to be saved, it will not be by the old minds with new programs but by new minds with no programs at all."

Daniel Quinn

Join me for a Morning Philosophy Circle favorite:

A long time ago in a forest kingdom not so far away lived a tribe of caterpillars. Their leader was big and fuzzy. So that was what they called him. Big Fuzzy. Now these caterpillars did what caterpillars do. EAT! And eat they did! As they munched about the forest kingdom, Big Fuzzy would walk around and profess, "Good Caterpillars! That's It! Keep eating! Keep eating or we'll die!" And this is how life was in the kingdom.

Until one day two caterpillars began to talk. "Hey, my grandmother told me a story that some caterpillars know how to fly. Wouldn't that be amazing?"

"Yeah, but we live on the ground and if we stop eating we'll die."

Another caterpillar that was only a leaf away joined into the risky conversation, "I heard a while back that Forest Fairies have seen them and know where they live."

"Well, that means they do exist and right here in our forest!" continued the first little caterpillar; "I am going to ask Big Fuzzy about this."

Off she crawled, munching the whole way until she arrived to the leaf that Big Fuzzy was devouring. "Excuse me, Big Fuzzy?"

"Yes...*munch*...what is it? ...*munch, munch*..."

"I'm wondering sir, well, I heard that there are caterpillars that can fly..."

"NONSENSE! ...*munch*... Keep eating! ... *munch*... Or We'll Die!" ...*munch*...*munch, munch*...

"Well, yes sir... but...well...my grandmother says she heard of them and one of the other caterpillars says the Forest Fairies know about them"...*munch*...

"NONSENSE...*munch*...I'LL GET TO THE BOTTOM OF THIS! NOW Keep eating! ... *munch*... Or We'll Die!"

Big Fuzzy *munch*ed his way to the middle of the forest kingdom and called out, "...forest fairies. Forest Fairies! FOREST FAIRIES! COME HERE AT ONCE!"

Sparkling colors filled the sky as three little fairies fluttered through branches down to where Big Fuzzy was *munch*ing. In unison with the pitch of morning songbirds, "Yes, Big Fuzzy, what would you like?"

"Now Forest Fairies ...*munch*...what's all this nonsense about...*munch*... flying caterpillars...simply ridiculous!"

"Oh, Big Fuzzy, It's true! It's TRUE! When would you like a turn?"

"Now wait a minute! ...*munch*... A turn? You mean to tell me I could fly?"

"Oh yes Big Fuzzy! All you have to do is climb to a high place, crawl into darkness and stop eating! It's that easy!"

"WHAT?! Now, let me get this straight. First I have to climb to a high place? But, but, but caterpillars are of the ground! Then I have to go into darkness. Which of course, is ridiculous because everyone knows caterpillars are afraid of the dark. And finally you want me to stop eating? But I'll die. I'LL DIE!" ...*munch*......
munch...

"Oh Fuzzy, It's actually quite easy."

"NONSENSE! I'm going back to make a proclamation that NO ONE is to have contact with you fairies and that everyone must keep eating OR WE'LL DIE!"

"Poor Fuzzy!" the forest fairies sang as they flew off.[4]

It is at this point in the story I usually ask my students what kind of ending would they like for the story. Interestingly enough, not one student has ever wanted the story to end with the caterpillars staying caterpillars of the ground forever destined to *munch*.

There really is no magic trick to getting someone interested in learning. On the contrary, the challenge I faced at TEMBA was finding ways to get people to unlearn all the ways they were taught to obstruct their own innate desire to learn. All the "Big Fuzzy" voices that told them they couldn't, shouldn't, or can't, when all along something inside was telling them they could. I, too, had my own "Big Fuzzy" voices of "This will never work. You'll fail and the children won't learn." I heard those voices every day walking into the classroom. To counteract them I placed a card on my desk that said, "Those who believe it can't be done, should

---

[4] Jack Von Dornum gifted me this story in the oral tradition in 1995.

not interrupt the ones doing it." It was my reminder that I was indeed doing it.

In actuality, when I first started TEMBA I was not sure how to explain what I was doing or what kind of classroom was being created. My pre-TEMBA days had brought me to the realization that learning is a life-long, limitless, creative process. My simple hope in education is to inspire people's willingness to engage whatever ignites their own authentic expression in order to support a diverse, peaceful and sustainable world. And honestly, even as I write this, I am still not sure how to describe what happens in TEMBA classrooms.

The first questions parents or potential supporters had were, "What's the curriculum?" and "What's the TEMBA program?" Usually after stumbling through, "well, ah, well, TEMBA is an integrated educational program…" or "…TEMBA has an alternative curriculum", I would be asked a question that continues to baffle me, "What's a typical day like at TEMBA?"

At TEMBA, since we were all in the practice of connecting to what is alive within ourselves and engaging the learning process wherever the path took us, each day was so radically different. I once asked Hudson, the student who wrote part of the forward to this book, "How would you describe a typical day at TEMBA?" I was hoping for an answer I could start giving to people. He responded with a 9 year old's giggle, "Yeah, right, Catherine. Is this a trick question?"

For years I have exhausted myself trying to answer these questions with coherent cognitive answers, often finding that I use way more words than anyone enjoys, and my guess is that people probably leave wishing they had never asked. Saying TEMBA has no set program, no set curriculum or even that every day is different is very risky. People equate that to chaos, as they understand chaos. Typically this chaos involves stereotypes of children. People misunderstand children to be beings that, when given the opportunity, will do whatever they want all day long, only making choices based on preferences, not on needs, and eventually become violent. The story goes that without rules to control the preferences, children will never learn basic skills. This invites rebellion, leaving us with an educational system where we're trying to enforce learning. Interestingly enough, there were studies done during Kennedy's administration that revealed that literacy was higher before "compulsory education" began in 1852. There has been a steady decline in literacy in the U.S. ever since.

Misunderstanding chaos is exactly what elicits fear in people who believe it is best to control and maintain obedience among children. In current systems of educational thought there is an underlying myth. Taught consciously and unconsciously, this myth says that humans are naturally flawed, lazy, violent, disconnected and selfish. This myth instills the belief that we cannot truly trust ourselves to know what would feed our own development and that somehow we must always look outside ourselves for the discipline to learn.

"A list of specific rules and consequences establishes a confrontational tone; the message is not that members of a community will work together and try to help someone who stumbles, but that anyone who violates a pre-established edict is in trouble."

Alfie Kohn

Containing education within these myths and stereotypes of children inhibits the inherent motivation for learning that humans naturally choose when the environment nurtures choice. Educational structures that set themselves up to try to control behavior or enforce learning invoke the anticipated chaos of rebellion, which exhausts educators.

Humans need choice; namely we all need the freedom to simply choose to learn. Without that innate internal sense of choice, human beings tend to rebel against "what" or "who" seems to be removing their choice. Then the energy of the student is focused on the rebellion instead of on learning. In this way the educational programs become focused on controlling the rebellion energy rather than feeding the energy that wants the choice to learn. When these patterns become pervasive, we see the all too familiar "power over" structure. People using systems that make more rules, punishments, rewards and trying to have "power over" the teachers' and students' behaviors increases the rebellion and resistance that they are trying to thwart. As long as we see systems in place where one group of people have "power over" another group of people we will continue to see an increase of violence.

Rebellious behavior is an indicator that something longs for change. The change that is crying out is the voice of choice to be heard, trusted, and understood. When a caterpillar has formed its chrysalis and the final transformation into a butterfly is complete, the insect knows the perfect moment to emerge from the sac. If anything or anyone tampers with the sac or tries to assist the creature's release from the chrysalis then the butterfly will die. It is imperative that the butterfly release itself; for through the movements required to break through the sac, the insect's

> *"We are born into the world like a garden that has been sown, but the seed must be nurtured and nourished by the appropriate environment."*
>
> **Joseph Chilton Pierce**

neural system gets the programming it needs to fly. The process can be perceived as quite chaotic from the outside, yet a beautiful order emerges.

Like caterpillars are hardwired to become butterflies, humans are hardwired to learn. What they learn will depend upon the external environment surrounding them. What they need to learn will depend on their internal environment. Children need to be seen and understood for being able to unfold into their fullest potential, a potential that includes an internal yearning to choose learning. If we create educational environments that support humans' natural choosing, then the unfolding of learning arrives with instinctive maturation and intuitive order.

" This kind of freedom made learning interesting; we were shown that knowledge isn't limited to the classroom, it's everywhere. TEMBA gave me a genuine love for learning and a need to always expand my views about the world I live in."

Eve Penberthy, 16

The way I am using the word "choice" is often misunderstood in a way which further fuels the uncomfortable sense of chaos experienced in most school systems. This idea of choice is most often confused with "meeting preferences" rather than "meeting human needs". So when we create a structure to educate, we need to consider this vital element of "true choice" within a learner or in a group of people. It has been my experience that humans "choose" to meet needs but they are often met with systems, and people, trying to meet preferences. When, as educators, and as human beings, we bring our focus to meeting needs, we access the kinds of choices that serve life itself. All moments become utilized for learning and chaos in its true nature reigns, allowing perfect order to unfold.

Mia, a 16 year-old, technically in attendance in my class at a South San Francisco High School, was going to her cell phone, by my account about every sixty seconds, checking and leaning low to listen. Offering a lecture at the chalkboard I, of course, believed to be the most important thing in the room, I continued to repeat my request to have the cell phones off during our time together. If I had taken action based on "my preference" to have her turn the cell phone off, likely I may have leaned into "school rules" to send her to the office or write her up. Having a student on her cell phone was not part of my lesson plan, but I made the gated, barbed wire fence that surrounded this school my reminder to connect before educating.

Mia would give me a nod and then, back to her phone. In my frustration I requested that she step into the doorway if she wanted to continue as I was finding it hard to concentrate watching her check her phone. (I asked for the doorway because another rule in this school did not allow students in the halls between classes. It would result in a citation.) Mia nodded again, stayed in her seat, and continued the behavior.

The rest of the students, now distracted as well, were beginning to chat. In this moment of chaos I chose to accept, listen, and empathize. While the volume of the chatting rose, I self-connected to my frustration and asked myself honestly if I just want to get my way or if there was a need motivating me. I connected to my need for contribution. This was my last day with these students and I really wanted to give them what I came to bring because I believed it would help them in their lives.

Feeling more present, I offered my own self-expression, loud enough to grab the class and cease the chatting, "MIA, I feel frustrated and sad we are spending all this time dealing with you on your phone when this is my last day to share with ALL of you. I want the phone off so I can trust I have your full attention, actually MY full attention to what we are here to learn. What do YOU need to have ease and willingness to turn the phone off and give your attention to class?"

"F*** IT! Catherine!" She was speaking loud enough for the classes next door to hear. "I'm trying to stop my cousins! Remember, you said, 'If you do what you have always done, you will get what you have always gotten? – well, f*** it, I'm tryin' it different. I've got to call it off!"

Connecting to Mia in my heart, it was easy now to see the cell phone as a strategy for safety and protection. Talking further, we learned she was trying to stop a "take out" of a boy who had pushed her on a bus the day before. The boy wasn't part of her "family." In this neighborhood, "take out" means kill and "family" defines who belongs with what group. I offered to go with her to the "take out" place after school if she wanted support. That touched her so deeply she dropped into her tears. The class and I sat with her. She wanted understanding for her desperation to stop ALL the killings she knows about and her hopelessness as to what she could really do about it. The whole class gave her understanding simply by listening. Then she and I role-played how she could talk with her cousins about her concerns.

> *"Do we want only to control short-term behaviors, or do we want to help children become responsible decision-makers?"*
>
> **Alfie Kohn**

All in all, the entire time the class and I spent with her, from the time I finally self-expressed myself instead of 'trying to control the situation', was less than 10 minutes. Then, the rest of the period was regular class.

If we rest into the chaos, connect honestly with ourselves about whatever the situation is stimulating in us (Respect Self), then we can connect honestly with our students (Respect Other). Whenever we are telling ourselves "they have to" or "we should," we enter the "power-over" structures trying to control the chaos. The gift of connecting is we find the heart of the matter inside the chaos and can attend to that. The sooner we create connection the sooner life becomes more fun and we engage the learning process. What student can concentrate on any subject if they are concerned with a murder that is about to happen?

Connecting to the needs alive in me, rather than the preference to continue my class without interruption, I contributed to the empathic connection between teacher and student. As important as it is to empathize with the student, it is equally as important that a teacher self-empathize. All needs matter and are vital to the connection and in the classroom. Building these empathic connections, resting into chaos, feeds the "power-with" dynamic in the classroom. The feedback I got was that she did get to her cousins at lunch and all "was cool." She let me know that she now felt stronger to speak when she knew of "things goin' down".

The complexity of creating an educational program where there is no set agenda and no set preferences, essentially requires a high level of comfort with true chaos. My understanding of chaos is that there is an underlying order inherent in all people, things, or situations if we look closely. As an educator seeking

"We are born for cooperation."

Marcus Aurelius

to create real choice and awaken learning, it is therefore my job to listen, observe, and then validate that underlying order, even when it seems random. And that really, is a typical day at TEMBA. We find order that is inherent internally within each learner, and then point to patterns that emerge for each student's learning style. Then, over time, we can begin to see patterns that emerge within the group dynamic. We experience freedom to choose to learn with guidance from the people within the classroom. We discover order out of chaos.

In order to support the intrinsic choice to learn within students, TEMBA set up a true multi-age classroom of children ages 5–14 with no grade levels. One of my inspirations, Vietnamese Buddhist peacemaker Thich Nhat Hahn, asks us to change our question from "What's wrong?" to "What's not wrong?" We at TEMBA discovered an aspect of "what's not wrong" with the American educational system originally in place – the one-room schoolhouse.

"There were no grades in the beginning, simply children learning at their own pace, something which may very well have been an advantage over today's system. Certainly, the benefit of having children older or more advanced than others helping those struggling or at lower levels of achievement, was preferable to some school situations now faced in cities where classrooms are overcrowded, teachers overworked, and students under-assisted."[5]

TEMBA did not set an agenda, specific pattern, or program, for children to fit into, rather we allowed patterns, or programs if you will, to unfold. This multi-age classroom allowed order to emerge from a true sense of chaos. We named the pattern, or program after we saw it. During the second year of TEMBA we had twice as many students as the first year, including two younger students who were four years old. We were noticing a bit of a challenge with organizing ourselves for classes because

---

[5] from "One Room Schoolhouses", *John's History of Education*, www.historyeducationinfo.com.

we did not have some general terms to refer to age groupings of students. I was adamant that I did not want to use grade levels.

I was worried that referring to the students or where they were academically on an arbitrary scale would invite in the rebellious system that I wanted to change. I wanted to shift the thinking implied by grade levels about what children 'should' know and knowing it by what 'grade level'. Grade levels tend to set up a learner to think that they are either 'ahead' or 'behind' something or someone. And that something or someone is vague. Criteria for where students are to be academically are decided based on the latest legislation or board whose interest is not always to see students actually unlock their natural learning, but rather have them obey and have test scores appear a particular way.

Grade levels also give rise to extrinsic competition. When learners are placed together with learners of the same age, the implication is that they will all be able to do exactly the same thing. And again that thing is decided by some outside force that is not actually connected with the individual learner.

When a learner is "skipped a grade" or "held back" the esteem of the student is what suffers. How can one skip an arbitrary setting or be held back because somehow they do not know enough? Students know exactly what they need to know to be alive. Outside forces determining the intelligence of a being is simply for domination of those beings – nothing more. So TEMBA did not have predetermined grade levels.

> *"I have a great belief in the fact that whenever there is chaos, it creates wonderful thinking. I consider chaos a gift."*
>
> **Septima Poinsette Clark**

As chaos ensued in our multi-age classroom, I started to feel a little exasperated and wanted some ease. One day when I was trying to help organize the students, the process of organizing was taking longer than anyone enjoyed and I was concerned that we were losing valuable class time. The older ones were going to work on some math skills with me, the youngest were headed to work in the garden with the science teacher and others were going to a music class.

The unease was quite apparent in my voice and face. Zach, six years old at the time, said to me, "Hey Catherine, I know something that's easy." Now, when Zach was this age and he was about to spout profound wisdom he would point his right pointer finger in the air as if he were the leader of a small nation. I learned quickly that when that finger was up, I was to listen. He continued, "Well, since TEMBA is a lion why not have the kids under seven be Cubs, kids up to 11 be Lions and everyone older be the Pride." His finger went down, he smiled at me, that was that, and the kids went their merry way.

Zach was referring to our school symbol. When I was fourteen, my sister gave me a book called *White Lions of Timbavati* because I had a fascination with African lions. This story documented the real white lions that had returned to South Africa. The white lions were thought possibly to be extinct, so the birth of these cubs was exciting not only for science but also for the people of

"So many things are possible as long as you don't know they are impossible."

Mildred D. Taylor

South Africa. I was taken with the story because the white lion is to many peoples in South Africa what the white buffalo is to many peoples of North America– a symbol of abundance and positive change.

One of the lion cubs documented in this book was named TEMBA. TEMBA is a Zulu word meaning hope. The name was chosen because the people's hope was to have more white lions return and stabilize in population. This book that my sister gave me traveled through life with me and was still on my bookshelf when I was designing the school I aspired to open.

TEMBA seemed to be the obvious name for the school since my hope was to create an educational program where students could practice peace and nonviolence, which I believed were things we already knew how to do but somehow had forgotten or set aside. My hope for education was to return to engaging the learning processes, a return to ways of peace and the creation of many more schools with this intention.

TEMBA does not have grade levels, but for ease of communicating about different age groups we have Cubs, Lions and Pride. Over the years, the ingeniousness of this orderly 'system' which arose out of the chaos of the first two years became even clearer. Zach was able to point to a pattern that was emerging out of the chaos and name it in a way that really serves the students because he was connected to his own choosing to learn and engaged with the learning of the moment. He named the order emerging from the chaos in respect to how the name itself would meet the human needs alive in the classroom. The title he gave to each age group is a natural progression rather than something that has to be earned. And certainly it would be impossible to be 'held back' or 'skip ahead' to any level with such a natural order.

Creating a learning environment that nurtures the choice to learn, empowers children to cultivate their intuitive sense of order and intelligence. Because every human being is a unique individual, this development happens at different paces. The multi-age classroom, and all

its chaos, nurtured an environment
of varied learners accessing their
intuitive sense of order. When
younger students saw older students
writing and reading, an internal
switch went on and they decided

*"Amidst chaos there is
harmony, and those who are
prepared will catch the tone."*

Vivekananda

that's what they wanted for themselves. When older students were
reminded of the unlimited imagination of younger students an internal
switch went on and they decided to put more dedication and creativity
into a project. Each student could birth their own 'final transformation
into a butterfly' by knowing their own perfect moment to emerge.

Sometimes all students would gather together for a particular
class. When all the ages were together I simply requested different things
of different students. For example, during sacred geometry lessons where
students copied notes from a flipchart and learned to construct a
particular piece of geometry I wrote on the flip chart in two colors. One
color would be for students who wrote in cursive and the other would be
for students who wrote in manuscript. For students just learning to write
the request was for them to copy whatever inspired them and mostly to
listen in as they drew pictures. All of this information was placed in their
journals, a book they were building for the entire school year.

One day we were in a sacred geometry class learning about the
Three. I had placed the words: Three, Trinity, Triad on the flip chart as a
title for our chart and discussion. As I was talking about the three
emerging from the one and the two I looked at a student's work. May was
six years old, new to writing, and the only request I had made of her was
to draw pictures. What I saw on May's page was a neatly organized
heading with the words, Three, Trinity, and Triad, written clearly in
cursive. I smiled, placing my hand on her back, "Wow, May, guess you've

started learning your cursive letters, eh?" She smiled and nodded yes with absolute delight. Children really delight in what I call "learning on the sly". They love learning a new skill and then surprising you with it. When there is room for children to explore skills and decide for themselves to pick them up, they ignite their own aliveness around learning.

> *"If you hear a voice within you say "you cannot paint," then by all means paint."*
>
> **Vincent Van Gogh**

When I am asked, "How do you motivate a student?", I answer, "I don't!" I never know who's going to inspire whom to learn or what will ignite interest in a particular learner. That is part of being comfortable with true chaos. I remain humble to the unfolding process.

Stephen, who joined TEMBA during its second year as a school, was only interested in the outdoors and things that could be built by hand. His mother expressed some concern about reading since he was now five and did not seem to display any desire even in learning the alphabet. I encouraged patience with his learning process. As he already could use power tools and construct with hammer and nails, it seemed to me that he was developing other skills and brain functions first, and we would see reading open up at a different moment in time.

When Stephen was seven he was in his third year at TEMBA having learned the alphabet but still was not terribly curious about reading. We now had a few new Cubs that were five. One of whom, Jake, had been unlocking his reading abilities from a very young age. His mother would joke, "Jake was born with a book in his hand."

During a Cub/ Lion reading group session Jake asked if he could read first. I said sure. The book I was working with had a part for the "teacher" to read and a part for "the student" to read in response. Jake, five years old, read the "teacher's" part without hesitation, precise inflection, and then looked up to wait for someone in the class to respond with the "student's" part, of course.

I giggled silently to see Stephen's response. He literally had his jaw on the floor in awe of Jake's reading ability. Stephen then looked at me and asked, "How'd he do that?" I smiled and said, "I think because he was ready. Are you feeling ready to learn to read?" He said, "Yes." In the next three months he unlocked the entire code and was reading everything in sight.

Out of absolute curiosity and mostly for my learning process about why reading unlocks at different stages for different students, one day in the hall I asked Stephen, "What pushed your willingness to read? Why was this year different from last year?" He explained that when he heard Jake read what he called the "adult" part he realized he would not have to wait until he was older to read "good" stuff. He had it in his mind that kids were only to read boring, slow things while adults got to read exciting things. He had simply decided to wait.

Sometimes when the waiting stimulated my worry or concern for a student's learning process I would express this to my student. As an equal member of the learning community, it is important that I validate my experience so that I can offer guidance to my students. Listening to my own need to contribute to their learning, I can clearly state my concern in a way that creates an empathic connection with my students.

Harry, eight years old, was zooming through his multiplication and division facts. When he "stalled out" between the numbers seven and eight, I had first thought it was a standard pause because I have noticed a natural rhythm to slow down here before with students. When a few weeks passed and I didn't see the progress I had hoped for, it stimulated my concern.

I really wanted to contribute to Harry and his learning process so I self-expressed, "Harry, when I see that you've been waiting on learning your seven, eight, and nine math facts, I feel worried because I want to help you learn. I had imagined you getting into long division before too long and I don't want you to hold yourself back. I also don't want to push you unless a little push would be helpful. Is there something going on or something different I could do to make it easier to practice these facts? "

He took quite a moment of silence before responding, "Will I have to sleep alone now?"

This was not what I had expected or anticipated. Who knew sleeping arrangements had anything to do with multiplication facts? So I inquired with sincere curiosity, "Could you share more about that?"

"Well, if I learn all my facts, that makes me older, then I'll have to sleep in my own room."

"Is this something you and your mom have talked about?"

"No. I just figured when you're old, you sleep alone."

"I'm hearing how it is confusing to be growing and learning so much, and at the same time you want to make sure you're still your mom's precious boy."

"Yeah, I am not ready to sleep alone."

Harry, his mom, and I had a meeting. Harry got a chance to express his concern. They worked out sleeping arrangements that worked for everyone in the house. Harry was in long division within the month.

By my taking responsibility for the need to contribute to Harry's learning and expressing my worry, Harry was able to reveal his concern around his need for safety. When all needs can be seen and met, then each member of the community can thrive.

Each person in the school has varying bodies of knowledge based on experience. The "power with" structure allows each student to bring their own set of experiences to class, awakening the inherent order within themselves and within the group dynamic. How the experiences are brought forward will vary. Experiences shared, whether students' or teachers', enlivens the human needs of learning, community, diversity, connection, companionship, expression, and equality.

My experiences at TEMBA have led me to understand, discover and see certain patterns in learning that occur when empathic connection takes a primary seat and "power-with" is the structure we strive to create. We discovered order that served life for us in our classroom. It became easier each passing day. The children really led the way. Anything that is in place now that we can point to as TEMBA grew from the students' chaotic evolution. I learned that children learn in hundreds of varied ways, so education must support fluidity and flexibility to meet the individual learner. Meeting the individual learner means designing programs that have no fixed ideas about children, and no set agenda about what will happen.

When I invited you to be curious and be undetermined, what I really meant was be curious to discover the patterns that will emerge from chaos while being undetermined about what the patterns will look like.

One year a group of TEMBA students turned the Big Fuzzy story into a play. They had Big Fuzzy return to the forest kingdom and actually make his proclamation that speaking of flying caterpillars is forbidden and to keep eating or everyone will die. What they demonstrated for their whole community was the rebellion that occurs when someone tries to block the natural maturation of any being. What ensued on stage was a rebellion led with drums. They had also studied that year how African slaves used drums as a communication tool to take over ships, plan rebellions, and organize escapes. They decided they also wanted to share some American history in the play, so they utilized drums.

With Big Fuzzy convinced through African rhythms, they all became butterflies. They performed a magical dance of transformation that showed the precise order that emerges from dark, scary, chaotic places. The students wanted the audience to learn what they had learned that school year – that everyone has a destiny, a calling of something most beautiful.

5

Tantrums, Terrorists, and Truth

"If we nurture our children, if we teach them and love them, if they can enjoy the harmony and freedom past generations fought for, they will lead us to a world free of prejudice and fear, free of hunger and poverty."

Nelson Mandela

When the school was at the St. Vincent's location in San Rafael, California, I commuted each morning along a magnificent drive called Nicasio Valley Road. It wound through hills and old redwood forests. It gave me thirty minutes to self-connect and catch up on worldly matters by listening to one of my favorite reporters – Amy Goodman[6].

This particular morning I was feeling especially engaged in life as the night before had been what I considered a huge success for TEMBA. Every school year the parents were encouraged to attend trainings in

---

[6] Amy Goodman hosts a daily independent TV/ radio news program called *Democracy Now!* (*www.democracynow.org*)

Nonviolent Communication^{SM} in order to support their family connections, to have understanding of how their children interact at school, and to build the TEMBA community. We were one week into this school year and the night before I had offered training in Nonviolent Communication^{SM} to all the TEMBA parents, and I mean ALL. It was the first time that EVERY parent turned up for training, including a few grandparents. I felt such excitement that this was going to be TEMBA's breakthrough year to have all families align in compassionate action and deepen practices of nonviolence as a community. I was thrilled with the potential outcomes and how the parents could effectively support one another this year. I was daydreaming into bliss about the perfect nonviolent year of school when I heard Amy Goodman's voice interrupt my vision. "OH, MY GOD!" her voice exclaimed through the airwaves. I turned the volume up on my car radio.

I listened as Goodman described how a second plane was now headed into the other tower of the World Trade Center. "Second plane?" "What is happening?" I said aloud alone in my car. I continued to hear the story unfold as it was actually happening – that indeed the twin towers in New York City were collapsing fireballs with people diving to their deaths. It is one thing to practice nonviolence in the comfort of community where all are willing to practice, it is quite another thing to practice when the world comes bombing.

> *"Nonviolence is the greatest force at the disposal of mankind. It is mightier than the mightiest weapon of destruction."*
>
> **Mahatma Gandhi**

Arriving to the front doors of TEMBA on the morning of 9/11, I shook with doubt. "Could I sink into this one?" I asked myself as I turned the key in the door. Behind me, running up the corridor, four children exclaimed, "Did you hear about the bombs?"

I took a big breath, turned around, and said, "Before we talk, let's first be clear about what we are talking about. Would everyone like to come in and take a breath with me?"

By the time we got inside a couple more TEMBA families arrived and we all stood in the library, by the Peace Elders wall, to discuss what to do. We were sharing the bits of information we had heard on the radio while driving to school and were in the process of canceling school for the day when Annie, nine years old, jumped in with her voice – "I sure hope whoever threw this tantrum gets heard so they won't need to do it again to get heard."

I remember pausing in the moment when I heard Annie's voice. We, adults, had been discussing the short term solutions for the moment all related to our immediate safety (which of course was purely related to speculation about what might happen the rest of the day), and this child offered a simple statement that fully embodied the possibility of true peace. Annie was already listening for the unmet needs in whomever was behind the towers coming down. She was already observing that if people hear the unmet human needs they might be able to help get those needs met peaceably. Without implying blame of any kind, Annie simply validated that what happened was a strategy for someone trying to be heard. She empathized that "whoever threw this tantrum" would like to be heard and understood. By saying, "so they won't need to do it again", she also empathized with all of us in our fear around the events that had just taken place. Annie understood that what had just happened did not serve life for anyone, including the ones who chose to do it.

"We can bomb the world to pieces, but we can't bomb it into peace."

Michael Franti

We decided to cancel school that day so that families could be together and decide how they wanted to receive the news of 9/11. I decided that the next day, our day of learning would begin with Annie's comment, so we could embark on the journey of understanding and maintaining our practice of nonviolence.

While driving back to my home later that day, I recalled another fateful event that was broadcast around the world. In February of 1990, I lay snuggled in my bed in the early AM hours, listening to a live broadcast from Robben Island, Capetown, South Africa. Nelson Mandela was being released from twenty-seven years of imprisonment. He had been locked up for his beliefs of equality and freedom. I had followed news of South Africa and her struggle to end apartheid for years. I had paid particular attention to Nelson Mandela's life as he went from choices in violence to choices in nonviolence in fighting to end apartheid. I had been falling in and out of alertness that early morning listening to the radio when the announcer said, "And now Mr. Mandela pauses to hug the guards as he leaves..." This woke me up in many ways.

Nineteen ninety eight brought me an extraordinary opportunity to travel to South Africa. The journey took me to a Sunrise Peace Ceremony on Robben Island. Robben Island, once a penitentiary for those who opposed apartheid, was now a museum for reconciliation. Ahmed Kathrada, a man arrested the same night as Nelson Mandela and served twenty-eight years for his beliefs, was now the curator for the museum and our guide for that morning. Ahmed walked us to his cell, then to Mandela's cell. I looked through the bars to the 4X6 room where these men slept for 16 years on

> *"To understand our capacity for nonviolence, we must understand our capacity for violence."*
>
> **Mahatma Gandhi**

the concrete floor with only a blanket until a hunger strike afforded them a cot for the remainder of their time. The memory of my warm bed where I first heard of Mandela's release entered my thoughts and stood juxtaposed with the stark concrete in front of me. I just had to ask, "Did Mr. Mandela really hug the guards good-bye when he was released?"

Ahmed told me that they all did. "Reconciliation is the only way," Ahmed shared. "Everyone must come out winners or else all lose." He further explained, "the triumph of the human spirit is to recognize in each other that there are no opposing sides, no prisoner, no guard – only coming together."

Later that same day in 1998, I attended an audience with the former first president of free South Africa, Nelson Mandela – the same man whose

> *"We cannot change the world until we create within ourselves the kind of world we want to live in."*
>
> **Marshall B. Rosenberg, Ph.D.**

cell I had stood in just eight hours prior. Someone in the audience asked Mr. Mandela – "How do we overcome our differences?" He replied with a simple ease and grace, "We must strengthen every choice and be responsible to the point of no return until forgiveness, compassion and understanding become habit."

As I write this now, I recall feeling fear that blame would be the national response to 9/11 and, in my own fear, began blaming people for how they would respond. I feared that other peoples' responses would create more violence. In all honesty, blame emerged first in me, as habit. Blame is an intricate game of denying responsibility. I fooled myself into thinking I was compassionate because I did not want to retaliate with bombs. But in my thinking that people were not going to be compassionate in the way I wanted, I missed the opportunity to really hear what was going on for others. The truly compassionate response came from a nine year old. It was Annie who offered the first empathic guess that historic morning. I asked myself, "What habit will you embrace in the coming days?" I wanted to be the kind of person that would hug the guards, the kind of person that will overcome differences with a habit of forgiveness, compassion, and understanding.

Arriving home with my thoughts still whirling about the morning, I got a phone call. Briar Pastoll, co-founder of The McGregor Waldorf School in South Africa shared, "We're in London until the United States allows air travel to resume," letting me know that David, the fourteen year old student traveling with her, and she were safe. I had been planning on picking them up at the San Francisco airport later that night.

My visit to South Africa in 1998 included the wonderful opportunity to work with teachers and students at the first Waldorf school in the village of McGregor. I had been invited through mutual donors to both TEMBA and the McGregor Waldorf School. The donors wanted me to share how I worked with Nonviolent Communication[SM] in the TEMBA classroom. Although apartheid had ended, many of the systems in South Africa, even alternative schools, were still infused with foundations in prejudice, blame, and punishment. Some teachers I met still utilized corporal punishment, thinking that it was useful at times to hit a child. I want to be clear that these teachers, like myself, only used the tools available to them until new possibilities presented themselves. All the educators I met at McGregor had a profound dedication to their work, wanting to bring peace and learning into the lives of every child. Their school also had the unique situation of being linked to an orphanage that gives sustaining support to children orphaned by AIDS. Getting to work with this school furthered my understanding of how blame continued separation and how reconciliation came through empathy and understanding.

The teacher of the sixth grade, or sixth form as they called it, invited me to come work specifically with them. She told me that they had many on-going conflicts, particularly between her and the students. In Waldorf education, a teacher stays with their class through every grade. This style allows the teacher to bond with their students developing trust with a growing relationship year to year. TEMBA had adopted this idea so the students could build community with their teachers and the teachers could really know their

"I'd rather play hug o' war.
Where everyone hugs instead
of tugs, Where everyone
kisses, and everyone grins,
and everyone cuddles, and
everyone wins."

Shel Silverstein

students. This teacher at McGregor Waldorf was not looking forward to continuing with her class into the next year, and indeed was quitting.

I entered the classroom with a little trepidation because my mind was lost in thought, "What am I doing in South Africa teaching about nonviolence when I wished that South Africa could be teaching the whole world about reconciliation?" And, I only had forty-five minutes with this class to share what TEMBA did to resolve conflicts.

We began with a game called "Do you ever wonder...?" The game is set in a circle of chairs with one less chair than the number of players. The person in the center asks, "Do you ever wonder about..." and they finish the sentence by saying something they wonder about like: whether butterflies ever eat butter, or whether animals really understand what we say to them, or who thought of milking the first cow, or anything else that pops into mind. Then, all the players who have ever wondered about that same thing get out of their chairs and run for a new chair. Since there are less chairs than players, one person remains in the center. That person now asks, "Do you ever wonder…?"

With this particular class, after we were well on our way with imaginative thoughts and lots of laughter, I shifted the game. I asked that we now make statements about getting our need for respect met in the class. I asked them to think of things people did or said that met their need for respect. Then the person in the center said, "My need for respect is met when…"

After several rounds of describing respect we quite naturally drifted into a discussion about what had been happening in the class. The students all made comments about what the teacher had been doing that they did not like. Some students commented about each other or about themselves and how they had not been following the rules. The teacher made comments about what the students had been doing that she did not like. When people began speaking simultaneously I interjected, "I feel very sad and worried that we might not find a way out of this situation as long as we continue thinking in the ways that I have been hearing."

> *"When you blame others you give up your power to change."*
>
> **Robert Anthony**

The comments were reflections of what everyone thought of one another. These ideas had become fixed in each person's mind. The teacher saw the students as "unruly," "misbehaving," "not caring about learning," and "disrespectful." The students viewed the teacher as "boring," "not able to do her job," and they viewed each other as "not able to listen," "disruptive," and "rude." The blame thinking had begun to create fixed ideas that kept them from really connecting to the feelings and the needs that were present in the situation.

Blame escapes solution, disconnecting us from the heart by seeking out what is right or wrong. It basically gives us two options. Blame our selves or blame others. This thinking can make conflicts last generations, as we have seen over and over again, throughout history. In South Africa, there was no need for further explanation of generational blame.

The class looked at a third option: take full responsibility for one's own thoughts, feelings and actions. We then took about twenty minutes to translate the blame thinking and the fixed ideas into what needs were alive in each person in the room. The teacher discovered she really wanted more caring connections with her students. She also wanted to contribute to their learning and acknowledgment for her knowledge that she was bringing to class. The students uncovered needs for clarity with communication, respect for the wisdom they brought to class, and understanding for the stresses of caring for the younger kids at home or at the orphanage. Identifying the needs led to all sorts of creative strategies to get all their needs met. One I particularly liked was to have a quick "check in" at the beginning of class. They proposed that they would go around in a circle and each say aloud one 'need' word that expressed what was most alive for that individual. This would give everyone a chance to be heard and to be seen for what was really going on before settling into study.

After my time with them, the teacher still had two more subject periods with her students that day. She was feeling a little nervous to be left alone again with her students. She shared that she was worried that the class would just go back to their 'old way of yelling' at each other, but nonetheless was ready to try a new way of connecting. I was delighted when she came up to me after school and was very excited. She said, "That was the best two hours I've had with my students all year!" She also informed me that she was not going to quit. I asked her to send me an email the following year to tell me how it was going.

Three months into her next school year she did email me. She reported that they began the year with what she called a 'needs circle' where they defined how they would all enjoy being together in the class to meet needs for respect, trust and safety with one another. She was enjoying her class and her class was enjoying her. As she stated in one of her emails, they had "formed an alliance for learning." That was true nonviolence and reconciliation. They transformed the blame and judgment into aligning their values, reconciling the connection, and moving forward together.

TEMBA and the McGregor Waldorf school had become "sister schools" as a result of that visit. Briar and David had waited in London after 9/11 until U.S. planes were no longer grounded. They arrived four days later, just hours before David was to perform *Shelter and Shade* to the TEMBA community, his one act play of a boy's journey of being raised by an African village. This was no cliché. A village, the McGregor Waldorf School, had indeed raised David.

Though Monday saw all the TEMBA families investing in connecting through learning Nonviolent Communication[SM], Tuesday's events brought our community face to face, on the most profound level, with habits of fear and blame. David's Saturday evening performance reminded us that our school, our village, had to look at how we could come together to raise our children in a world where adults threw tantrums big enough to kill thousands of people at a time.

The fear infused by 9/11 played out this way – one parent threatened to report another to Child Protective Services; one parent was extremely upset that the children were talking about the events at school because she wanted to preserve her child's innocence (in fact, she tried to sue the school based on this premise); one parent who believed war was necessary did not know how to reconcile that belief with keeping her student in TEMBA; one parent was angry with me for "being too soft" in my response to 9/11; two parents were frightened that the books TEMBA was choosing for the children to read were promoting violence; and several parents wanted the children not to go out for the weekly hikes because they felt we were no longer safe. As some parents were defining who was a 'terrorist', others were placing American flags on their cars to not be 'profiled.' We may have all attended the training on how to communicate nonviolently, but fear had stimulated the habit of blame. I had complete sympathy for that sixth grade teacher at the McGregor Waldorf school. I was contemplating quitting just to give myself a sense of peace.

Whomever came up with FEAR being an acronym for False Evidence Appearing Real must have been enlightened. Nothing could have more accurately described how the people around me were responding to 9/11. With only thoughts and enemy images to go on, people were speaking and taking action that led to more misunderstandings and disconnection. The events of September 11, 2001 tested my ability to maintain my values as a teacher whose educational philosophy was rooted in nonviolence. The following is part of a letter I

> *"True security comes not from defeating enemies but from not having any; from turning enemies into friends."*
>
> **Buddha**

sent on September 23, 2001 requesting a meeting with all the parents and teachers of TEMBA:

> We are living in an auspicious time. The choices ahead will be challenging, yet enlightening. I am calling all the teachers and parents together to pose some difficult questions and hear each other about how we can thrive as an educational community. I have had many individual conversations with TEMBA parents since Sept. 11. Each conversation has revealed the depth of reflection each of us are having about how best to support our children, and how to live our lives as parents and as Americans. These conversations have reflected fear, confusion, and anger.
>
> The children have been reflecting the same sentiments through their play. Children integrate intensity the best way they know how – mimic the adults, play with their toys, and act it all out.
>
> Here is some of what I am hearing the children say: "I am sad all those people died;" "I feel like the world is ending;" "Even school feels unsafe now;" "My parents are scared and that makes me scared." Through an all school circle we came to agreements to make TEMBA a safe place to play. The children need many avenues to express their feelings about what happened and their feelings about the impending war our government wants to make. I believe they are longing for the protection that humans can provide one another through LOVE. I believe they want to grow, thrive, and learn, without the stress of further violence.
>
> I am asking us to come together to discuss our tangible differences of beliefs and how we intend to hold them all in respect in these difficult times. We need to come together to re-commit ourselves to an educational institution whose foundation is rooted in the words of Mahatma Gandhi, "We must be the change we wish to see."

Last week in one of the parent discussions, I was told, "Catherine, you live in an ideal world." I agree with this statement. From my perspective, people do not have to suffer, humans do not need labels, children do not need to grow up fast, learning is a life-long process, anger ignites compassion instead of vengeance, gardens grow healthy food, all living beings are seen as equal, viable members of a community, and there is no discrimination among peoples based on age, gender, skin color, choices, abilities, or spiritual beliefs. I do not consider this ideal. I consider this TEMBA.

We did meet as a school community, a village, and gave voice to our fears, differences, and challenges. We were able to transform enough of our blame into needs that we would like to meet to enable movement forward as a group. In the cases of emergencies created by our government or other groups of people, we came up with tangible plans to deal with them. Part of this discussion resulted in two families deciding to leave TEMBA.

This discussion truly tested us as a community in our practice of nonviolence. Transforming blame so that we could move beyond acceptance of differences to completely embrace all expressions of humanity in the room that night pushed our own personal evolution as humans. Moving beyond acceptance to an invitation of different ideas, opinions and ways of being gave us the opportunity to be the village we wanted to be raising our children in, a thriving community, dependent on a diversity of people, thoughts and beliefs. By

"In the end, nothing that ever caused one pain will exist."

St. Catherine of Siena

committing to this practice of nonviolence as a group each of us requested of ourselves an immense amount of resolve and responsibility. This asked each of us to self-reflect, empathize and take ownership of all our behaviors. It called upon our humanity so that we would listen deeply to each other's needs, invoking the utmost creative power for resolution.

A parent commented later that same school year that she had always convinced herself that people need to have the same ideas and beliefs to be a thriving peaceful community. She found that TEMBA not only challenged that idea but her experiences at TEMBA showed her that it was in the differences that growth and sustainability were found. The families that chose to leave did so as a means to truly meet their own needs. They stayed connected to TEMBA families in other ways. The years that followed 9/11 continued to push the learning curve for all of us as a community and as individuals.

During the 2003 school year, the students put together a video project asking youth how they felt about the United States bombing Afghanistan. The project was initiated by Tammy, a student who wanted more input from people her own age because she was extremely confused about all of the world events. Tammy said it this way, "I don't actually know what I think. You, my teacher, believe that bombing won't bring peace. My

> *"Our ability to reach unity in diversity will be the beauty and test of our civilization."*
>
> **Mahatma Gandhi**

father says it is the only way to get things settled. And my mother, says she doesn't believe in war but sometimes it is just necessary."

Tammy interviewed students from other schools, kids off the street, and other TEMBA students. She discovered a variety of ideas and by the end of the project decided that she was still unclear about her own opinion of world events. What she did discover, and stated as part of presenting the video during TEMBA's End-of-the-Year Performance, is this: "I still do not know what I think about the war, but I know I want to be kind and human to the people around me."

In 2007, TEMBA supported Jiva Manske, Jesse Wiens, and myself to bring Nonviolent Communication[SM] through a day of art to kids in Afghanistan. Forty-one kids in Kabul got the opportunity to experience a day of TEMBA. This, of course, was the first TEMBA classroom I had taught in that was protected by real guns just outside the window. While traveling in Kabul, we were only allowed in United Nation secured buildings, which meant armed guards. I would greet the guards with a smile and think about Tammy's statement that maybe I still do not know what to think about war but I wanted to be kind and human to those I met. My heart was tender with humanity. That day was rich with giving and receiving. We sang, drew, painted, colored and played, connecting at the human needs level. We had created a country within a country for a day. A country where no one got in trouble or punished and all were treated equal with a chance to express their own aliveness. We had created a country with laughter, joy, safety, ease, harmony, community, belonging, inclusion, inspiration, creativity and happiness. While just outside our "borders", outside the windows of the building, men stood in their country armed with guns. The reminder that not all had learned that there can be more fun and effective ways to meet human needs.

> *"Through its emphasis on deep listening – to ourselves as well as others – Nonviolent Communication fosters respect, attentiveness, and empathy, and engenders a mutual desire to give from the heart."*
>
> **Marshall B. Rosenberg, Ph.D.**

That day in Afghanistan brought together children from schools, from the streets, and from a local school for the deaf. The day began with an African gathering song, during which everyone stood in a circle and learned the words and the movements. Then, the Afghan children received necklaces gifted and made by the children at TEMBA. The rest of the day was spent exploring nonviolence and the universality of human experience through art projects.

After imagining our perfect life and getting a list of human needs, Jiva led the children on an art journey involving crayons. Do you remember your first moment in life picking up a crayon and marveling at transforming your page into colorful life? For each of these forty-one Afghan children, regardless of age, it was their first time. Jiva asked them to choose the needs most alive for them in their vision of a perfect life. Each need they chose would be represented by a different color. They colored until the page was filled and resembled the life they wanted. Then we gave out black crayons. Jiva asked that they now completely cover the color until all they could see was black on their page. Jiva suggested that covering the color in this way represented how sometimes things happen in life that make it hard to connect to the life we want. When he asked what some of those difficult things might be, they mentioned family members dying, bombs, and arguing. Now with the black encompassing the entire page, we asked that they take the edge of a pencil and create a new picture through peeling away parts of the black. This new picture revealed the color beneath. We saw clearly now in the art that the needs were still there beneath the conflict, that the life we want is always there and within reach. At the end of the

"If we are to make progress, we must not repeat history but make new history."

Mahatma Gandhi

day a twelve year- old girl put it this way, "What I learned today was that life is not going to stay in one condition. If there are some sad moments, then after that, a hundred percent happy moments will also come."

As an educator, as an American, and as a human practicing nonviolence, it was important to me to go to Afghanistan. I wanted to connect face to face with the humans on the land where my government was dropping bombs. I wanted to represent the people I had known over the years at TEMBA who wanted peaceable change and support to come to the people of Afghanistan. I wanted TEMBA's experiment in Truth to reach the hearts of Afghan people. And, in fact, I heard first hand what Annie had already guessed that first day – that everyone really wanted to be understood and to have the tantrums stop.

TEMBA's educational philosophy in nonviolence is intimately connected to the interdependence of all humans – when one suffers, we all suffer, or when one chooses to courageously heal the pain, we all have an opportunity to heal. TEMBA

> *"Love is the cure, for your pain will keep giving birth to more pain until your eyes constantly exhale love as effortlessly as your body yields its scent."*
>
> **Rumi**

responded to 9/11 by tangibly engaging the learning of transforming blame, dissolving fear, and cultivating compassion. It is a revolutionary act to resist giving into fear and separation in order to offer empathy and understanding to one another. When we seek understanding we find the human behind the pain. When we take action connected to the needs that are desperate to get met we form new alliances. We begin to create a new history. Schools have the potential to be a center point for building strong communities – for being the village that raises the child. The kind of schools we create will define the kind of world we will live in.

6

∿

A, B, C's and 1, 2, 3's

"My alphabet starts with this letter called yuzz. It's the letter I use to spell
yuzz-a-ma-tuzz. You'll be sort of surprised what there is to be found once you
go beyond 'Z' and start poking around!"

Dr. Seuss

When TEMBA first started, we had renamed 'recess' to 'Free Play',
but the name itself still had the same effect as the title 'recess'. It
gave parents the uncomfortable feeling that this was time spent "not
learning" and students responded to the title as if this was the only time of
the day that they had "free choice" in learning. 'Free Play' became
'Integration Play' because that is what play is – it integrates our
experiences so that we can learn skills for life at the deepest level.

Joseph Chilton Pearce, who was a teacher at the Jung Institute,
said, "Play is the only way the highest intelligence of humankind can
unfold." I agree. When the mind has time to wander and imagine, the
brain then has the space it needs to integrate skills learned; the emotions

can find their expression and the spirit and intellect can determine if the skill is necessary to serve life. I once had a student ask me why we listed the needs for 'learning' and 'play' separately. The student was referring to the "Tree of Life" we built for the classroom. Our tree was made from paper, wood, and fabric. It stood tall above all as a reminder of the language of needs. We built the trunk of the tree with bark which had needs words written on it. Each piece of bark had a different needs word on it. We placed the needs here because we decided that needs were the life force flowing through, sustaining us like the sugars that flow through the xylem and the phloem just inside the trunk of a tree. We placed feeling words on the leaves because, like leaves, feelings change constantly. So when I answered the students question, the only answer I came up with was, "I guess we, and I think I mean adults, forget they are the same thing."

> *"It is paradoxical that many educators and parents still differentiate between a time for learning and a time for play without seeing the vital connection between them."*
>
> **Leo Buscaglia**

Integration Play was listed like any other class, a regular, necessary part of the daily curriculum. And boy, did we need this class to sort through skills, emotions, and ideas about 9/11! On the Wednesday following 9/11, the students completely directed the play: towers built with blocks were crashed down by flying blocks, a 'care-unit' emerged with some students needing nurturance and empathy for the loss of loved ones, and a game of tag erupted with enough energy to power a small city. That morning, Integration Play was followed by a circle. The students clearly articulated their feelings and needs and we came up with agreements to keep TEMBA a safe place for all. The play had given the students time to integrate experiences so words and ideas could be clearer.

Play was an essential part of the curriculum at TEMBA because it allowed the learner to integrate his or her whole being – physical, emotional, intellectual, and spiritual. Gandhi once said that if he were to decide, children would not be instructed to read until they were ten. Because children express themselves in hundreds of ways, he saw it as a disservice to limit children's expression to the one form the government had chosen for communication, writing and reading of the language. Gandhi believed that children are close to the authentic expression of God. He suggested that we have children draw, paint, play, build and create what God wants us to hear. If we allow space for the children's authentic expression, we engage them as a whole human being – physically, emotionally, intellectually, and spiritually.

> *"A bird doesn't sing because it has an answer, it sings because it has a song."*
>
> **Maya Angelou**

Physically, students develop fine and gross motor skills. The awareness and development of their physical being affects their interactions with themselves, others and their environment. Understanding strengths and limitations in the body create a deeper awareness of one's interdependence with one's environment.

Intellectually, students process information. This is the ability to recognize and pursue an idea or question that originates in the learner, meeting an innate need for order and learning. The intellect is our ability to follow a set of procedures and produce something unique thus meeting needs of choosing one's goals and expressing the meaning of one's life. Our intellect gives us the ability to take information into the future and apply, integrate and teach it, satisfying the need to self-express one's authenticity.

Emotionally, students assimilate reality and protect their needs. The emotional body is a path to self-knowledge that guides the learner's moment-to-moment decisions. Creating a learning environment with a curriculum that supports learners' needs for empathy, love, safety, belonging and trust provides a practice ground for students to become decision makers, choosing effective strategies not only to meet their own needs, but also the needs of others. An effective curriculum helps a child develop self-awareness while guiding them to become an integral member of the community.

Spiritually, students strive to express their authentic presence. I like the way Martha Graham puts it:

> "There is a vitality, a life force, a quickening that is translated through you into action, and there is only one of you in all time, this expression is unique, and if you block it, it will never exist through any other medium; and be lost. The world will not have it. It is not your business to determine how good it is, not how it compares with other expression. It is your business to keep it yours clearly and directly, to keep the channel open. You do not even have to believe in yourself or your work. You have to keep open and aware directly to the urges that motivate you. Keep the channel open."

When learning invites the whole child to participate – intellectually, emotionally, physically, and spiritually – then education becomes a relationship to life itself. The curriculum itself is then based on meeting the authentic human needs of the learners rather than "meeting standards." Students can engage in connection with others, move through conflict, have a sense of self in relationship to others, express ideas, understand others' ideas and relate to the world around them.

In 2004, TEMBA relocated to a valley beneath the 14,179 foot peak of Mt. Shasta. Snow was inevitable. One day the students were delightedly more interested in the snow pouring out of the sky than our previously scheduled project. So, we went outside. We built a snowman. Not just any snowman, but a seven-foot snowman that required constructing a ramp in order to put the middle section of body and the head into place. A student commented, "This stuff sure is sticky."

We returned inside to answer the question – why was snow so sticky? Why could it be made into gigantic shapes? We explored the molecules, design, and chemical structure of a snowflake, discovering its structure is based in the number six. When we further explored molecules we learned that carbon is also based in six. That led to the awesome discovery that we are carbon based life forms. We found excitement in being connected to snowflakes through the number six so we created geometric designs based on six, then explored counting by the number six. The beauty of the connection inspired art so we composed six syllable silly words to describe snowflakes and our selves. We wrote six line poems to express our feelings about winter. And so went that day at TEMBA. It was better than my initial plan. Granted, I already knew we are carbon based life forms, but that's the beauty of beginner's mind – I get to learn it anew every time.

> *"Education is not something which the teacher does. It is a natural process which develops spontaneously."*
>
> **Maria Montessori**

A fully integrated curriculum based on human needs offers students a chance to explore subjects at their natural pace for learning. Allowing students to investigate subjects concurrently uncovers the interdependence we have with all life. Rather than teaching subjects independently of one another, TEMBA linked academic skills through themes that were meaningful to the students, engaging their whole being. In the case above, snow became the theme that engaged the learners and guided us through the academic material.

Children need respect for their authentic presence. Sometimes, as with most five-year-olds I've met, this authentic presence wants to explode things. This is because humans have such a drive for learning that they enjoy to take things apart in order to understand them. Also, a big mess is a lot of fun! This drive to take things apart also wants to know how things fit together. Science and Mathematics are the exploration and naming of all patterns in the world, in us, how it all fits together, and how it all comes apart. Mathematics and its related fields offer such an opportunity to engage the whole learner, inspiring a deep rooting in self-awareness and self-love. It allows us to connect to something beyond ourselves with clear understanding that we are a part of the BIG something.

> *"All the world is made of faith, and trust, and pixie dust."*
>
> **J.M. Barrie**

Children need this life's existence validated. This validation stimulates the wisdom already there in the child – connecting them to meaning and purpose in life. When we understand we are a part of this world we become more invested in contributing to life. We value the connections that exist and we expand the possibilities to discover peaceful ways of coexisting not only with other humans, but all life forms.

I am amazed and saddened when I witness educational systems that seem to unknowingly train everyone to 'hate' math and girls to internalize the message that they cannot be good at math. I am hopeful that when we connect to mathematics as a means for students to meet their need for belonging, we can end 'math phobia'. The way we teach anything, including math, can greatly affect a student's self-esteem and sense of belonging.

While at San Francisco State University, I took a course entitled Mathematics for Elementary School Teachers. On the first day of class the professor asked us what stage (grade) of math we wanted to teach. All the students yelled out "kindergarten" or "first grade", while I raised my hand. "And you, what do you wish to teach?" he asked me.

I replied, "I'm not sure exactly why, but my first thought is algebra because it seems it would be the easiest."

He laughed and said, "Yes, and here's why." He went on to explain how typically everyone wants to teach beginning math subjects because they think that it would be easier. Indeed, simple calculations may seem easier but what everyone forgets is that at the very beginning you are naming concepts and learning a new language. This is much more complex than algebraic equations, unless of course, the math phobia has been installed in the learner. He explained that a math phobia comes from students being taught math in rote methods and in a way that implies that they should memorize answers rather than discover them. Rote learning only engages the temporal lobes of the brain, which is used for short-term memory. The student may learn the math facts long enough to get from test to test but in the long run will remain confused about the concepts and how one process leads to the next. So, in the next class he taught us all an entirely "new" system of numbers so that we could remember what it was to walk in the shoes of kindergardeners and first graders. This professor offered me inspiration not only for my own personal learning but also for how I would in turn educate others. I thought at the time that, if we wanted a nonviolent society, and one of the ways to achieve that was for people to develop equanimity and understanding of each other, why not begin with math?

TEMBA's foundation for mathematics was Sacred Geometry. Students learned in the old mystery school method – with compass and straightedge. Beginning with the shapes of the numbers, students took their time in noticing patterns without the pressure of memorizing facts. This method clearly instilled a confidence in math, whether or not a student decided math was their personal passion. Recognizing the patterns in life that we see, feel, smell, hear, and touch uncovers the qualities of numbers. Exploring the meaning behind the numbers helps us to understand why the world is structured in the way it is and assures us of our placement in the world. When the students would construct forms with the straight edge and compass that they recognized in the world around them, they would feel peaceful and know that they belonged in the world.

Every year we would begin with a circle, the One. Immediately, the need for belonging is met with the simplicity, the accuracy, and the excitement of an exact circle created with the compass. Our first art piece each year was to imitate the tree and construct our age in the form of concentric circles. Holding one point of the compass still at the center point while the arc is drawn fully around with the other point of the compass, we simply changed the distance from the same center point – letting our age emerge on the page like rings on a tree. Children never tired of this exercise. In fact, they enjoyed returning to it year after year to see how they had grown. Coloring in the rings became a kind of meditation to reflect on their life.

I recall one student, thirteen at the time, had taken quite a long pause on her fourth ring. Holding a few colored pencils in her hand I thought she might have been deciding which color to use. As she continued simply to stare at her page, I asked, "Was there something about that age in your life?" She looked up at me and said, "Oh yes, my brother died when I was four. I was trying to remember his favorite color."

Children need respect for the authentic expression of their whole being, even if the task at hand is math. At TEMBA, we engaged the learner at an authentic level of understanding – as a whole human being meeting their needs in a way that is in service to all. This kind of learning validates the learner's belonging, meaning, purpose, and contribution to life.

During the first ten to twelve weeks of school we would encounter the numbers one through nine by learning their construction with the compass and straightedge, and building their solid equivalent. This work with constructing the numbers allows a learner to relax and develop what is innate in themselves. As forms unfolded on the page or in their hands, the students began to see with a deep sense of understanding how the numbers, patterns of nature, appear in relation to their own being. The

> *"I have things in my head that are not like what anyone has taught me - so natural to my way of being and thinking."*
>
> **Georgia O'Keefe**

numbers then simply become symbols, a language to speak of all things that live in our universe. The language becomes something that acknowledges our existence. Math is no longer separate from us – the learner, a whole being, is now interacting with a language that can help them to understand themselves and the world around them.

In Sacred Geometry, it was fun to note that not only did the symbol for numbers came from constructing and understanding nature's forms, but so did our written language. When I was first experimenting with my ideas, I was still working in a public school system. One day I was working with a five-year-old student after school who was struggling in her classes. I was told that she could not read or even recognize, remember, and write the letters of the alphabet. I showed her how to use the compass and straightedge. Together we constructed a twenty-four pointed geometric shape. Her excitement grew as we drew each line. We connected each point on the circle to every other possible point. It looked something like this:

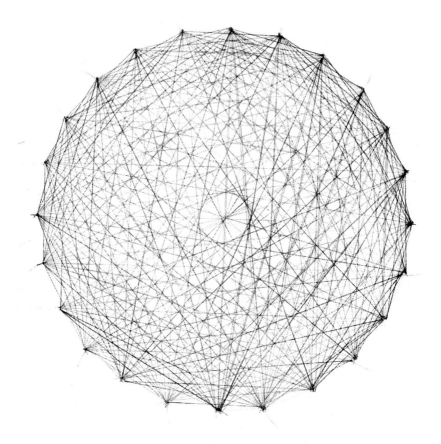

I said, "Let's just look at it for a moment and see what the design shows us." She began to hop up and down in her seat as she saw "A," then "B," and so on until she had found every letter of the English alphabet. I said, "Wow, you saw the whole alphabet."

She was so excited she began to trace the letters in the geometry piece then rewrite them free hand on another piece of paper. It is important to note that I did not have a fixed intention of getting her to practice her alphabet; I simply wanted to make an authentic connection. I invited her to explore the possibility to gain confidence in the motor skills in her hands. I was open to whatever would have happened. After she pulled all the letters from the design, we then rearranged them into the order the alphabet is usually taught in and began to play, creating two and three letter words.

I enjoy this example of geometry to engage learning because I truly believe something awoke inside her – quite literally something in the Broca's Area of her brain. She connected that the forms of the letters existed inside this geometric design because she was actively interacting with a language that defines the universe. She could relate to the shapes and easily pull out recognizable letters.

"It is more important to journey than it is to arrive."

Stephen Hawking

What was unknown, at least at a conscious level, was that her ancestors, humans who invented the written language, had probably discovered the forms in a similar way – looking in nature at natural patterns then mimicking those forms with lines and circles.

Dan, a seven-year-old student who had transferred from a local public school, announced during his first week of school at TEMBA, "You can't make me read!" Immediately, I let him know that I knew that I couldn't.

When we began the Sacred Geometry, he loved it. Dan, with ease, could create extremely symmetrical, complex, geometric images. I thought I noticed something about how he saw things, so I pointed it out to him, "It is amazing how you have the ability to see things forwards and backwards at the same time." Then I followed with my best empathic guess, "I imagine seeing things forwards and backwards at the same time can be frustrating when you are trying to read words. Would you enjoy practicing a lot of geometry to strengthen this skill before we even try reading?" He was delighted and now the pressure to read was completely off – at least at school.

"Do not train children to learning by force and harshness, but direct them to it by what amuses their minds, so that you may be better able to discover with accuracy the peculiar bent of the genius of each."

Plato

Thanks to the work by Rudolph Steiner, it has become socially acceptable, to some degree, to not have your child read until seven years old. Unfortunately, as we move into the new millennium with the Bush administration's 'No Child Left Behind' curriculum still in public schools, students are being pressured into recognizing their alphabet by age three and reading by age five. The current expected reading level for first grade is the same as what was expected of me in third grade, thirty years ago.

Dan left TEMBA when he was ten with reading skills intact, a confidence to decode words, and an unfettered willingness to learn. One day, as I was walking in the downtown area where we both still lived, Dan passed by me on his bike. Now fourteen years old, he yelled out to me,

"Hey, have you read Howard Zinn's *People's History of the United States?* You should check it out!" Now THAT is a huge book! I must admit that to this day, I haven't completely read every page.

Reading can be a joyful strategy to meet needs that are alive in the reader. I feel brokenhearted when I think about the extrinsic pressure placed on parents and children "to read." Over the years, I have witnessed the immense stress in each decision a parent makes to contribute to their child's well-being, safety, and learning. Parents are bombarded with "shoulds" from a culture that tells them: when their child "should" be reading; how their child "should" behave; what they "should" be purchasing for their child's happiness; who their child "should" grow up to be; and the list goes on. Unfortunately these external "should" messages become internal. I have found that, more often than not, parents and teachers get caught in the blame game, mostly blaming themselves. Chris Mercogliano from The Albany Free School in his book *Making It Up As We Go Along* puts it this way;

> And then comes the blame game. It's the teacher's fault for not
> teaching or expecting enough; it's the students' fault for not
> studying enough; it's the parents' fault for not caring enough; its'
> the country's fault for not maintaining high enough standards. Here
> is the voice of fear speaking, whose reasoning is always circular.

"our responsibility is no longer to acquire, but to be."

Rabindranath Tagore

At TEMBA, most of a teacher's time with a parent was centered around offering empathic listening and translating these "should" messages into needs for understanding. Imagine the alliances that could be created if parent conferences were changed from the game of "who's to blame" to a conscious connection of heartfelt sharing, building trust and understanding that ultimately supports the child's learning process. At TEMBA, we tried not to place parents, teachers, and students in opposition to one another in order to find fault, but rather all were seen as equal in responsibility to support learning and creating community. When blame arose we leaned into relearning the 3 R's.

Kodi, a nine-year-old boy, came to TEMBA having transferred from a public school with the labels of "angry", "dyslexic", "distracted" and "not able to focus". Seeing Kodi as a whole human being rather than as the labels provided to me, I discovered that Kodi's needs for creativity, movement, and play were not met with "traditional" forms of teaching children to read. I got curious; then, I got two crates of tennis balls.

On each individual ball I wrote a single sound picture so that all the possible variations of spelling for sounds were created. I first had him separate the balls into the two crates by consonant and vowel sound pictures. Then, I proposed that we create a ball game.

With sound pictures, when letters are placed together, they spell certain sounds. In the English language there are 44 phonic sounds that create what we say, but 127 ways to spell those sounds. 127! The sound oo (/u/) alone has 18 ways that it can be spelled. Now you know how many tennis balls were in the game.

" By education I mean an all-round drawing out of the best in child and man – body, mind, and spirit."

Mahatma Gandhi

In one game we created, I would throw as many balls as I could, as fast as I could, directly at Kodi. The balls Kodi actually caught would be placed on the floor in front of him, in the order he caught them in. Then he would sound out the nonsensical word and make up a definition for it. I was entirely delighted because he had invented a fun strategy for teaching students to decode words.

I like how Kodi spoke about his experience:

"When I got to TEMBA, I was not reading, I couldn't spell, and I couldn't write legibly. One day, Catherine assigned *The Golden Compass*, and it was a real book. It was an adult book and she assigned it to me! She said, 'Kodi, I want you to read this book.' I got through three chapters and then I just turned it on, I turned my reading on. Whatever she did, she set up the energy, the comfort level, so I could just feel comfortable reading. I enjoyed reading enough that I just whizzed through that book. And it was a huge book!"

I had assigned *The Golden Compass*, by Phillip Pullman, to Kodi when he was eleven. There was never any pressure placed on Kodi to start reading or make it happen. I like how he owns his own process by saying, "I just turned it on, I turned my reading on." If we take the opportunity to satisfy the needs alive in our learners, we engage their authentic creative expression and intrinsic motivation for learning.

We can create curriculums based on needs, inviting us to know our students and our selves as whole human beings. When we connect first to the human needs that authentically animate the life within us, we engage learning as a limitless, creative process. If we design curriculums that work to meet the needs of the student as a whole human being, then we will create a learning community that is peaceful, productive, and sustainable.

We can know peace in the classroom.

We will know peace in our world.

Peace and passion
Kindness and compassion
Let's teach the whole world
To jump into action

Love your brother
Help one another
Let's teach the whole world
To work together

Respect the planet
While we still have it
Let's teach the whole world
To get into the habit

Follow your heart
Trust who you are
Let's teach the whole world
To wish on a star

This was a song written by the students with their music teacher, Tom Finch, in 1997. The refrain would completely explode between verses with children playing air guitar and singing at the top of their lungs, "Rockin'! Rockin' Respect! Yeah!"

EPILOGUE

◈

Every Day is a Day of Hope

"All that we do must be done in a sacred manner and in celebration. We are the ones we have been waiting for."

Hopi Elders

One typically full Wednesday – after completing meditation, a history lesson, a Hula Hoop making project, lunch, dance class and a small romp through the snow, we were just settling into our seats to begin our calendar project. The calendar project allowed the students to build a calendar from scratch, sequencing the days and the months together numerically with art of their own creation for each corresponding month.

One five year old girl in the class was working diligently with her numbers when I looked over her work and saw that, in her delight with speed, she forgot the number six. That threw the entire sequence for the month off track. I shared this by simply having her see the numbers. We began to erase together when she just dropped out of her chair into a ball of tears on the floor.

I sat down beside her. She was completely laid out face down on the floor with tears flowing. I placed my right hand on her back, behind her heart, and said, "I hear so much sadness. You can just let it move through."

Another student, age seven, who had been sitting beside this child looked on with intense interest. By his expression I made a guess and asked, "Are you feeling a little uncomfortable with the big emotion in the room?"

He slowly shook his head "yes" as his eyes widened even more. Keeping my physical position on the floor with the little girl in front of me, and intending to also connect to him I asked, "Are there sometimes big emotions in your house?"

Hearing this the little girl from the floor responded with a "YES" that shook everyone's attention towards her. She continued to express verbally through her tears, "There's always big emotions ... when I am with my daddy I don't see my mom and then when I am with my mom, I don't see my dad for such a long time."

I reflected back what I heard and let her know that, if she wanted to, she could crawl into my lap for a hug when she felt complete. While she continued her grieving with my hand on the back of her heart, I reconnected with the boy who was now even more stimulated by the swell of emotion.

I asked him, "I am wondering if it is uncomfortable for you because you want so much for your family to feel peace with each other?"

He smiled slightly, shook his head "yes," and let out a big sigh of breath. He returned his attention to his work.

About one more minute of tears flowed, then the little one got up from the floor, crawled into my lap and said, "You know, Catherine, it wasn't about the numbers."

The class shared a unified giggle. I smiled in reflection of the sweetness and took in the wisdom of what I was witnessing. She smiled, gave me a strong hug, got up and returned to her work.

Thich Nhat Hanh shares that breathing and smiling together is peace education. I believe that taking the six minutes, like with this little girl, to offer space to be with what is alive gives us that much more space for our learning and living to take place. What if we returned to breathing and smiling in any moment that conflict emerged within ourselves or in our environment?

Every day is a day of hope. Every moment is a moment to practice peace. I am excited about the possibility of transforming our schools from mini war zones to communities of peace – places to practice nonviolence. My excitement for such a large scale transformation is that I trust it only takes the focus of the connection that is right in front of me at any given moment. One connection at a time, we can build the societies we want.

Years ago, Jack Kornfield gifted me this story:

There is a man walking by a river and he sees a baby floating in the water. He runs to the river and rescues the baby. As soon as he brings the baby safely to shore he sees another baby floating. He runs and rescues that one. As soon as he has that one safely on shore – two more babies. Then three, and so on. The question is –

When do you stop running to the river to rescue the babies and start walking upstream to stop whoever is throwing them in?

This story, with its unanswerable question, describes what it is to be an educator. I spent years running to the river. For me, TEMBA was walking upstream.

It was a difficult task to choose which stories would land in this book. I have so much more I could share – all the End-of-the-Year TEMBA performances where hundreds of people would gather to learn from the children; Community Meals, where the children cooked for their families and friends; Wild Days, where we explored the outdoors; the Luna Project, where we planted 1,000 redwood trees; Farming – how we grew organic food and lived on organic farms each year to help with planting, harvests, or the births of baby goats; Harmony Now, TEMBA's music program; Celebration Days, where we honored each child's birth and contribution to the community; Dancing Lodge, where we engaged our authentic expression through movement and Indigenous Peoples' traditions; how we studied history through the lens of nonviolence; and so much more.

I hope if you made it this far in reading my book, something has inspired you, ignited your own creativity, and connected to your authentic presence to become the change you wish to see in the world.

I hope that our paths cross. Then we can smile.

And breathe.

Together.

Thank you for walking with me.

Peace All Ways.

Appendixes & Resources

Appendix A

NEEDS

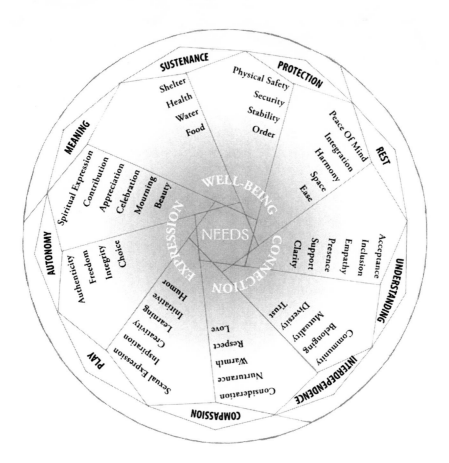

Universal qualities of our One Life together.

We can know this One Life through deeply hearing, voicing, and embracing Life's qualities, Needs, in each moment, in each expression of ours or another's.

(This is not a definitive list but rather, an example of what the word "needs" is referring to throughout this book)

Based on the work of Marshall B. Rosenberg, Ph.D., Manfred Max-Neef, John Kinyon, Catherine Cadden, and Jesse Wiens.

Appendix B

SHIFT HAPPENS

"POWER OVER"/ "POWER UNDER"	"POWER WITH"
Perceives Scarcity	Perceives Abundance
Denies Choice	Acknowledges Choice
Evaluates & Judges	Observes & Expresses
Blames Other/ Blames Self	Takes Responsibility for Feelings and Needs
Makes Demands	Makes Requests
Listens Selectively	Listens Empathically
Wants to be right	Wants to connect

"Power is of two kinds. One is obtained by the fear of punishment, and the other by the arts of love. Power based on love is a thousand times more effective and permanent than the one derived from fear of punishment."

Mahatma Gandhi

FEAR Paradigm	LOVE Paradigm
FORCE	LISTEN
ENEMY-IMAGES	OBSERVE
AUTHORITY	VALIDATE
REWARD/ PUNISHMENT	EMPATHIZE

Based on the work of Mahatma Gandhi, Marshall B. Rosenberg, Ph.D., Sura Hart, and Catherine Cadden.

Resources for Learning and Support

❧

PEOPLE

Catherine Cadden offers consulting, trainings, storytelling, playing with children, and would love to hear how you enjoyed this book.
Contact: **catherine@temba.org**

Gloria and R.D. Cooper
Educational Architects and founders of The New Age Academy, offering consulting, coaching, and trainings in Sacred Geometry and Creating Educational Blueprints.
Contact: **naamtshasta@msn.com**

Dominic Barter and Restorative Circles
Developing effective models and training programs to address youth crime and its consequences, as well as working with judges, school administrators, police, social services, youth and community leaders in supervising implementation.
Contact through: **www.restorativecircles.org**

Sylvia Haskvitz

A certified Nonviolent Communication trainer since 1989, offering workshops, trainings, and coaching for individuals, couples and families. Contact through: **www.nvcaz.com/tucson**

Jack Kornfield

One of the key teachers to introduce mindfulness and vipassana meditation to the West. His approach emphasizes compassion, lovingkindness and the profound path of mindful presence, all offered in simple, accessible ways in his books, CD's, classes and retreats. Contact through: **www.jackkornfield.org**

David Schanaker

Musical sounds that assist relaxing, having insight, and meditation. Contact through: **www.musichealers.com**

Michael S. Schneider

Educator and writer who encourages a love of learning through an appreciation of mathematics, nature, art and science. Contact through: **www.constructingtheuniverse.com**

Jesse Wiens and ZENVC

Supporting people to be completely, authentically human, both individually and in the company of others. Side effects include thriving, dynamic organizations; compassionate communities; strong, loving relationships; and lives of great meaning. Contact: **jesse@zenvc.org**

ORGANIZATIONS

The Center for Nonviolent Communication

Contact: **www.cnvc.org**

The Institute of Indigenous Arts/ SMI International

Contact: **www.iiainternational.org**

Kindle-Hart Communication

Kindling heartfelt interactions in families and in school communities.

Creators of the **No-Fault Zone** game.

Contact: **www.k-hcommunication.com**

NVC Academy

Nonviolent Communication[SM] learning from home with tele-classes and a whole lot more.

Contact: **www.nvcacademy.org**

Play in the Wild! Wilderness Initiations into Nonviolence

For youth and their families.

Contact: **www.playinthewild.org**

~ତୁ৹

BOOKS

A Path with Heart: A Guide Through the Perils and Promises of Spiritual Life, Jack Kornfield

A Pebble for Your Pocket, Thich Nhat Hanh

Beginner's Guide to Constructing the Universe: A Voyage From 1 to 10, Michael S. Schneider

Beyond Civilization, Daniel Quinn

Black Elk Speaks, John G. Neihardt

Boys Will Be Men, Paul Kivel

Compassion in Action, Ram Dass & Mirabai Bush

Destructive Emotions, His Holiness the 14th Dalai Lama and Daniel Goleman

Emotional Anatomy, Stanley Keleman

Ethics for the New Millennium, His Holiness the 14th Dalai Lama

Evolution's End, Joseph Chilton Pearce

Facing A World In Crisis: What Life Teaches Us In Challenging Times, J. Krishnamurti

Lies My Teacher Told Me, James W. Loewen

Long Walk to Freedom, Nelson Mandela

Nonviolent Communication; A Language of Life, Marshall B. Rosenberg

RESOURCES FOR LEARNING AND SUPPORT

My Life is My Sundance, Leonard Peltier

Making It Up as We Go Along: The Story of the Albany Free School, Chris Mercogliano

Peace Is Every Step, Thich Nhat Hanh

Punished by Rewards, Alfie Kohn

Real Boys, William Pollack, Ph.D.

Respectful Parents/ Respectful Kids, Sura Hart & Victoria Kindle Hodson

Speak Peace in a World of Conflict, Marshall B. Rosenberg

The Compassionate Classroom, Sura Hart & Victoria Kindle Hodson

The Essential Gandhi, Louis Fischer

The Homework Myth, Alfie Kohn

The Magical Child, Joseph Chilton Pearce

The Powers That Be, Walter Wink

Transforming the Mind, His Holiness the 14th Dalai Lama

Voices of a People's History of the United States, Howard Zinn

Walden and Civil Disobedience, Henry David Thoreau

Why We Can't Wait, Dr. Martin Luther King, Jr.

Zen Mind Beginner's Mind, Shunryu Suzuki Roshi

More on Books...

"I Can Read With My Eyes Shut!" – Dr. Seuss

At TEMBA, children worked with books in a myriad of ways. Children would have books at school that they would read themselves; a book might be assigned for independent reading that went to and from school; a book would be chosen to be read aloud at school to the whole group; and a book would be assigned to the parents to read to their child at home. The book the parents were assigned to read would be the same for every family. When the families were a chapter or two from completing the book, we would all gather at school in our pajamas for a "Read-In". The first few years we always did a "Read-In" on Dr. Seuss' birthday.

The following are just a few of the TEMBA favorites that inspired discussion for our principles in listening, observing, validating, and empathizing – not to mention, they are great stories read aloud:

A Golden Compass, Philip Pullman

Alice's Adventures in Wonderland & Through the Looking Glass, Lewis Carroll

A Little Princess, Frances Hodgson Burnett

A Wrinkle In Time, Madeleine L'Engle

George's Secret Key to the Universe, Lucy & Stephen Hawking

ISHI, Last of his Tribe, Theodora Kieber

Mrs. Frisby and the Rats of NIMH, Robert C. O'Brien

Number the Stars, Lois Lowry

Peter Pan and Wendy, J.M. Barrie

Roll of Thunder, Hear My Cry, Mildred D. Taylor

The Giver, Lois Lowry

The Hobbit, J. R. R. Tolkien

The Sneetches, Dr. Seuss

The Miracle Worker, William Gibson

The Never Ending Story, Michael Ende

The People Could Fly, Virginia Hamilton

The Secret Garden, Frances Hodgson Burnett

The Secret Life of Bees, Sue Monk Kidd

Watership Down, Richard Adams

THE REVOLUTION CONTINUES...

THE COMMUNITY MEAL COOKBOOK

Stories and recipes from the TEMBA School community meals.

Summer 2010

ENGAGING THE AUTHENTIC: NEEDS BASED CURRICULUM

A Practical Guide for Educators and Parents with activities, instruction, and themes from the TEMBA classroom.

Fall 2010

Visit **www.temba.org** for the latest information about these and other upcoming books by author Catherine Cadden.

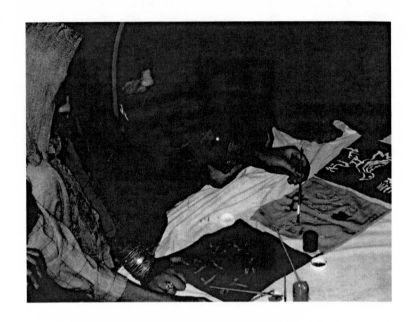

Would you like to see the life-changing work described in *Peaceable Revolution Through Education* on the big screen?

Filmmaker and eMotion Studios cofounder Glen Janssens is working on it! Footage has been shot and is ready for post-production.

If you are interested in giving to support the completion of this feature film, please go to www.temba.org or contact glen@emotionstudios.com.

CPSIA information can be obtained at www.ICGtesting.com

265716BV00001B/4/P